BUYING A
PROPERTY IN
BULGARIA

REVISED AND THOROUGHLY UPDATED 2ND EDITION
FOLLOWING BULGARIA'S ENTRY INTO THE EUROPEAN UNION

BUYING A PROPERTY IN BULGARIA

How to buy an investment property, holiday retreat, or home for retirement in this delightful and fast developing country

JONATHAN WHITE

how tobooks

Published by How to Books Ltd
Spring Hill House, Spring Hill Road,
Begbroke, Oxford OX5 1RX.
Tel: (01865) 375794. Fax: (01865) 379162.
info@howtobooks.co.uk
www.howtobooks.co.uk

How To Books greatly reduce the carbon footprint of their
books by sourcing their typesetting and printing in the UK.

First edition 2005
Reprinted with amendments 2006
Second edition 2008

British Library Cataloguing in Publication Data
A catalogue record for this book is available from the British
Library

ISBN 978-1-84528-215-8

Cover design by Baseline Arts Ltd, Oxford
Produced for How To Books by Deer Park Productions,
Tavistock, Devon
Typeset by Pantek Arts Ltd, Maidstone, Kent
Printed and bound in Great Britain by Cromwell Press,
Trowbridge, Wiltshire

Contents

'The future belongs to those who believe in the beauty of their dreams.'

– Eleanor Roosevelt

Acknowledgements

I would like to start by thanking Maarika for her support, understanding and encouragement throughout the months of writing this book.

In Bulgaria, I would like to extend my gratitude to Svetlan Bonev for his valuable contribution and for validating the tax sections of this book, to Maria Boneva for her input on various aspects of the buying process in the real estate market, Chris and Jain Goodall of Quest Bulgaria for sharing their experience of Bulgaria with my readers and to all the other people that have either directly or indirectly supported this project.

Without the support and encouragement I have received from many people I would never have had the courage to pursue my dreams in Bulgaria. To all those people I have met in Bulgaria – I would like to extend my grateful thanks to you all for sharing your thoughts, opinions, experiences and advice on Bulgaria.

Special thanks have to go to both Mila and Emil Ranguelova for the warmth and generosity that they have bestowed on Maarika and myself during our trips to Bulgaria.

In England, warm thanks to Ralitza Ranguelova for introducing me to Bulgaria in the first place, for her friendship and for her inspiring artwork (see Photo Gallery) and my thanks to Nikki Read and Giles Lewis of 'How To Books' for giving me the opportunity to share the joys of buying property in Bulgaria with the rest of the world. I would like to extend my gratitude to Nick Hutchins for checking through the manuscript, Katie Harker for her inspiring attention to detail during the editing process, Bill and Michelle Antrobus at Deer Park Productions, Pantek Arts for the typesetting and Mandy Preece for proofreading.

In Canada, I am grateful to Steven Dengler of XE.com for kindly granting permission for me to include details of their XETrade system for purchasing foreign currency over the internet.

Last, but not least, I would like to thank my old friend Lisa who always said that I should write a book one day – and to my mother and father for giving me the upbringing that has allowed me to benefit from the many splendid things in life.

About the Author

Jonathan White was born in the United Kingdom, graduating from the University of the West of England (UWE), Bristol, with a first-class honours degree in Systems Design. A couple of years after graduating, he looked to Malaysia for adventure and went on to spend almost six years living and working in Malaysia. Jonathan's passion for travel has also included trips to Thailand, Singapore, Taiwan, Indonesia and Australia.

Jonathan has worked in the IT industry for over 17 years, becoming a Chartered Engineer in 1998. During his career, Jonathan has enjoyed additional work-related travel to America, Spain, Hong Kong and India. He was once blessed with being in India coincidentally at the same time as Roger Waters (of Pink Floyd fame) – when Roger was running a one-day concert in Bangalore. With the help of Jonathan's friends in India, he was able to get a last minute concert ticket and enjoy possibly one of the best concerts of all time!

Jonathan first travelled to Bulgaria in 2003 – one of many subsequent trips. It was not long before he fell in love with the country and acquired a real estate portfolio and a passion to share his experiences with others.

With a growing interest in the country, Jonathan felt that there was a lack of information about buying property in Bulgaria. So, whilst on a flight from Sofia back to London, he decided to set about writing a book that would help others through the process – and hopefully dispel some myths along the way.

Now living in Bulgaria, Jonathan and his wife Maarika are running their business Inspired Ideas Ltd [www.inspiredideasltd.com]. Their business has a number of different strands to it, including real estate and information technology (IT).

On the real estate side, they provide a personalized approach to help clients find property in Bulgaria, as well as managing Varnarentals.com which allows owners and estate agents to advertise their Bulgarian rental properties.

On the IT front, Jonathan provides consultancy for a web-browser based information management system called Easy Information Management (EIM) developed by Excelpoint Ltd (UK). EIM is suitable for any business, with many 'out-of-the-box' solutions. For example, a Real Estate system for estate agents to manage their properties, clients, viewing trips etc.

His latest business venture is the development of PropertyDragon.com - a website that brings buyers and sellers of property from all over the world together. With an ambitious development plan, PropertyDragon.com provides a very simple, effective way of finding different types of real estate or rental investments anywhere in the world – with free registration, and all features for property buyers provided free of charge. PropertyDragon allows private sellers, estate agents and property developers to advertise their properties – with many value added services

In his free time Jonathan writes for property magazines, has co-authored a second book on Bulgaria ('Buying in Bulgaria', Apogee Publishing) and is working on his first novel. A love of photography prompted the start of FotoFriction.com – a stock photography website providing stock photos from different countries in the world, with particular focus on Bulgarian imagery for use in publications that require Bulgarian themes (e.g. websites, magazines, posters etc).

Preface

If, like me, you find yourself inexplicably drawn to Bulgaria's many wonders, then I hope you will find this book both a useful guide and companion as you venture into the world of buying your own home in Bulgaria. Whether you are looking to invest, retire or buy your very own place in the sun, this book aims to answer the many questions you will have about the whole buying process and more.

Bulgaria is attracting increasing interest from foreign buyers around the world – fascinated by its property investment potential, glorious stretches of golden sands and breathtakingly unspoilt nature. It's not hard to understand why so many private investors are drawn to Bulgaria, with its geographic location providing many alternative types of accommodation to suit all tastes – whether it's a mountain retreat in a ski resort, a seaside apartment, a country house, or a modern city-based apartment – Bulgaria can truly cater to all these requirements with ease.

When faced with the prospect of buying a home in Bulgaria, I tried to find as much information as I could on the subject – but lacked any real point of reference or guide. I found myself trawling the internet for information, finding conflicting details and no books or other published information focussed specifically on buying property in Bulgaria.

An important decision of this kind needs to be based on good research and ideally a feel for the kind of experience you are likely to have. After all, buying a home overseas is not for the faint-hearted.

My goal in this book is to provide you with exactly the information I was searching for myself when I was looking to buy property in Bulgaria. This should save you valuable time and hopefully prevent you from making costly mistakes due to a lack of information or guidance.

As one of several emerging markets in Central and Eastern Europe you may feel somewhat in the dark about how things work in Bulgaria. You will also, no doubt, have heard some horror stories about people's experiences. Like anywhere in the world, there are good and bad experiences to be had by all.

If you are reading this book as an investor, you are more than likely aware of the increased interest in Bulgaria – particularly in the real estate market. You will also be aware that the real estate market is not as developed as it is in other parts of Europe, such as France, Spain and the United Kingdom.

As an investor focussed on real estate, you may also be tearing your hair out in the frantic search for the best place to invest your money (or the bank's money!) Would I be right in thinking that some typical questions on your mind are:

◆ Should I invest in Eastern Europe?

◆ Is it safe to invest in Eastern Europe?

◆ Should I invest in Prague, because everyone else seems to be?

◆ Wouldn't it be better to invest in the northwest of England?

◆ Florida seems to be gaining in popularity, shouldn't I invest there instead?

Whilst this book does not answer these questions – what it does do is present you with information that will put you in a position of greater knowledge about buying property in Bulgaria.

As with all investments, you need to assess the risks, do your homework and when investing in real estate overseas, I would recommend that you visit the country and decide whether it's the place for you. Bulgaria may not suit everyone's taste, but does any country in the world? At the end of the day, it's your decision and your decision alone, despite what advice you receive from others on your journey.

If you are reading this book as a retiree (or with a view to retiring) and you are thinking about settling in Bulgaria, I have provided some practical information about living in your home, indicative living costs, visa information etc. Like investors, I would recommend that you seriously consider visiting Bulgaria and spending some time out there before deciding to emigrate for good.

If your motivation for buying a property in Bulgaria is as a holiday home for your family and friends, this book provides practical information on such topics as furnishing your home, managing the security, arranging bill payments etc. So, read on!

Whatever you do – don't despair! – over the next few chapters I will guide you through the process of buying your own property in Bulgaria, step by step. Together, we will look at the many questions on your mind and – based on the experiences of people I have met, my own encounters and various other sources – explore how these can be practically addressed.

If you are looking to buy land I will also provide you with some helpful information to help you on your way.

This book also includes an extensive appendix with several sample contracts. This is to enable you to familiarise yourself with the typical content of different contracts in Bulgaria. Do note that these have been provided in English based on actual translated contracts (with sensitive details amended), but for the notary deed to be legally binding in Bulgaria it does have to be in the Bulgarian language.

Please note that facts and figures in this book have been revised for 2008. Costs have also been calculated in euros using an average exchange rate of £1 = €1.47.

To complement your research of Bulgaria a list of useful websites covering various areas, such as estate agents, cable TV providers, internet service providers and accommodation can be found in Appendix H.

The Photo Gallery also provides a pictorial insight into the country, as well as providing examples of properties.

By the end of this book, I hope that you feel equipped to take the next step, and find your dream home in Bulgaria, whatever your motivation may be.

Jonathan White
January 2008
[jon.white@inspiredideasltd.com]

1
Why Bulgaria?

With so much investor interest in Bulgaria in recent years, it's not difficult to answer the question 'Why Bulgaria?'

I understand that each of you may be driven by different reasons for buying a property in Bulgaria – therefore, let me try to provide you with a comprehensive introduction to the factors that I think make Bulgaria *the* place to buy a property.

If you are looking for miles of golden sands; warm, sunny summer getaways; mouth watering original food; a plentiful supply of red wine; opportunities to ski; a wide variety of homes at considerably lower prices than the rest of Europe; then you will surely find that Bulgaria has a lot going for it.

Bulgaria enjoys a low cost of living and joined the European Union in 2007. For those of you who grow tired of the same old trips to the likes of France or Spain – Bulgaria offers a refreshing change of scenery and culture – and all within less than a three-hour flight from the UK!

What you must do, is first ask yourself, why do *you* want to buy a property in Bulgaria? Perhaps you haven't made your mind up yet, or you want to know more about Bulgaria before deciding? If so, then this chapter will provide you with an insight into the reasons why you might consider Bulgaria.

What's particularly attractive about Bulgaria is that it can offer you so many contrasting lifestyles all within the same country – whether it be an energetic ski down the mountain slopes in winter; a lazy, relaxing break in the country in the spring; a sun-bathing haven in the summer or a cosmopolitan city life in the autumn months – there really is something for everyone.

Do you want to be left behind, while others readily snap up the bargains on offer?

THE PROS AND CONS OF BUYING PROPERTY IN BULGARIA

One of the primary reasons I imagine you are reading this book, is to decide whether Bulgaria is a place where you want to buy a property. Before we delve into more detail, I think it would be helpful for you to understand what some of the pros and cons are when considering Bulgaria's property market.

Pros	Cons
Property is cheaper than many other parts of Europe, with houses[1] in some rural locations as low as 7,000 euros.	You cannot own a property with land as a foreign individual; you have to set up a Bulgarian company.
Good potential for future capital growth, with accession to the European Union (EU) in 2008.	Getting to Bulgaria is still more expensive than some other parts of Europe.
Diverse range of properties in cities, mountain ski resorts, coastal areas and countryside.	You may have to make a quick decision to avoid losing the property, with the increased interest in the region.
Land prices have more than tripled in some regions between 2004 and 2008p	Financing options may be more limited than if you were to buy in Spain or France, for example.
Recognised as an emerging property market, with potentially high rewards for the bold and the brave!	Alleged concerns over a two-tier pricing structure.
Improving infrastructure, with funds from the EU.	Roads, pavements and other areas of infrastructure are not currently up to Western standards in all areas.
Beautiful countryside and coastal areas – offering great locations for properties in unspoilt landscapes.	Water mains are not available in all areas – you need to check that it is available before you buy or build a well.
Increased exposure of the Bulgarian real estate market in the British media (e.g. 'A Place In the Sun', 'I Want That House').	The summer months are not as long as they are in some other European destinations such as Spain – lasting from May until September.
Flying time is only two and a half to three hours from the UK – making it perfect for weekend city breaks.	The buying process can seem daunting at first.

[1] Such houses are typically not up to Western standards and would generally be in need of major renovation.

KEY FACTS ABOUT BULGARIA

Let's take a closer look at some of the facts and figures about Bulgaria.

Official name	Republic of Bulgaria
Capital	Sofia
Population	7.6 million (2006)
Area	110, 994 sq. km
Religion	Eastern orthodox
Language	Bulgarian, English[2], Russian
Text	Cyrillic
GDP	$US 31.5 billion (2006)
GDP growth	5.7% (2006)
GNI per capita, Atlas method	$US 4137 (2006)
Unemployment	6.9% (Dec 2007)
Inflation	8.4% (2007)
Currency	Leva (lv) 1 Euro = 1.95583 leva
Average monthly salary	181 euros (2007)
Other major cities	Burgas Pleven Plovdiv Ruse Stara Zagora Varna
EU membership	Joined on January 1st 2007
Time zone	GMT + 2
International airports	Sofia (for the capital) Varna (for the coast and beach resorts) Burgas (for the coast and beach resorts)
Driving	Driving in Bulgaria is on the right-hand side
Internet users	2.2 million (2005)
Internet country code	.bg

[2] English is a common second language, which tends to be spoken more amongst the younger generation, whilst Russian is more common amongst the older generation due to the communist era.

WHERE IS BULGARIA?

Bulgaria is located in south east Europe, covering an area of approximately 111,000 square kilometres bordering with the following countries:

◆ Romania

◆ Greece

◆ Turkey

◆ Serbia

◆ Macedonia

CLIMATE

Bulgaria has hot, dry summers that tend to peak at 30°C – enjoying a summer season from May to September on the Black Sea Coast. The average air temperature in the summer is about 24°C, with a water temperature of 25°C. There are more than 240 hours of sunshine in May and September and more than 300 hours in July and August.

Bulgarian winters are cold, in extreme cases dropping to a temperature of –30°C in some regions (including the mountains) – with an average temperature of –1°C during the season.

Typical **average** daily temperatures:

	Jan	Feb	Mar	Apr	May	Jun	Jul	Aug	Sep	Oct	Nov	Dec
Sofia °C	−1	1	5	10	15	19	23	24	16	12	6	1
Varna °C	3	6	6	12	17	22	24	23	20	16	10	4
Borovets °C	−1	1	5	9	15	19	22	23	16	12	6	1
Plovdiv °C	1	3	7	12	17	23	23	24	19	13	8	3

BULGARIAN REGIONS

Bulgaria is divided into 28 regions (or provinces), which are located within 6 administrative divisions:

North West region	Vidin, Vratza, Montana
North Central region	Veliko Turnovo, Gabrovo, Lovech, Pleven, Ruse
North East region	Dobrich, Shumen, Varna, Razgrad, Silistra, Targovishte
South West region	Sofia- Town, Blagoevgrad, Kyustendil, Pernik, Sofia- District
South Central region	Pazardjik, Plovdiv, Smolyan, Kardjali, Stara Zagora, Haskovo
South East region	Burgas, Sliven, Yambol

PUBLIC HOLIDAYS

Date	Holiday
January 1	New Years Day
March 3	Bulgaria's Liberation from Ottoman rule – the National Day
March / April	Easter: One week after the Catholic Easter
May 1	Labour Day
May 6	St George's Day / Bulgarian Army Day
May 24	Day of Bulgarian Culture and the Slav Script
September 6	Unification Day
September 22	Independence Day
December 25–26	Christmas

COST OF LIVING

The cost of living in Bulgaria is currently amongst one of the lowest in Europe. With an average monthly income of 181 euros per month, this is not surprising.

It's not uncommon for two people to be able to eat out, with a main course, dessert and a bottle of wine, and still have change from a 10 euro note. In time, the cost of living will rise, but certainly for the next few years, prices are likely to remain comparatively low when compared to the rest of Europe as a whole.

The cost of a good bottle of Bulgarian wine costs about 2.50 euros, with beer available from as little as 0.50 euros a bottle.

Pensioners who have moved to Bulgaria to retire, from other countries (such as the United Kingdom) are spending, on average, 1,000 euros a month on their living costs. That's an annual cost of only 12,000 euros!

TOURISM

Bulgaria ranks among the top seven tourist destinations, according to a survey by TUI AG, one of the largest European tour operators.

It is estimated that up to 70 per cent of tourists venture to the Black Sea Coast in search of sand, sea and sun – the most popular period being between June and September.

With miles upon miles of sandy beaches, and hot summers – the Black Sea Coast attracts a large number of tourists every year, and this number is growing – with over 6.5 million foreign visitors in 2007.

Arrival of tourists from abroad to Bulgaria, by country, Jan-Sep 2007

Country of origin	Number of tourists
Austria	36 511
Belgium	34 467
United Kingdom	294 451
Germany	441 501
Greece	514 534
Denmark	82 680
Israel	89 276
Ireland	54 383
Spain	24 334
Italy	39 877
Canada	8 331
Luxemburg	2 403
The former Yugoslav Rep. of Macedonia	56 656
Netherlands	52 653
Norway	75 505
Poland	125 032
Portugal	9 272
Romania	595 568
Russian Fed.	197 726
Slovakia	103 985
USA	44 033
Turkey	32 316
Ukraine	53 091
Hungary	43 475
Finland	71 150
France	84 996
Czech Rep.	105 939
Switzerland	16 729
Sweden	97 700
Serbia and Montenegro	106 607
Japan	8 114
Iceland	6 590
Slovenia	9 910
Lithuania	5 732
Latvia	4 733
Estonia	6 496
Malta	3 975
Cyprus	13 265
Other countries	87 239
Total	**3, 641, 013**

Source: National Statistical Institute, Bulgaria (September 2007).

Tourism itself has been estimated to reach 12 million by the year 2020 based on research by the World Trade Organisation (WTO).

Bulgaria has many resorts on the Black Sea Coast, along 380 km of sandy beaches. In the north these include Sunny Beach, Albena, Golden Sands, Varna, Riviera, Rusalka, St. Constantine and Elena. In the south these include the ancient coastal towns of Nessebar and Sozopol.

So what other attractions does Bulgaria have to offer? There are numerous sources of healing mineral waters in Bulgaria with spas and healthcare clinics. These were established around a cultural heritage dating back to Greek and Roman times preserved in historical monuments, museum towns and monasteries.

The best-known spa centres are: Grand-hotel Varna at St. Constantine resort; Ambasador Hotel at Golden Sands resort; Dobroudja Hotel at Albena resort; the Burgas and Globus hotels at Sunny Beach resort; and the Pomorie Hotel in the coastal town of Pomorie. There is growing speculation that Bulgaria's health tourism will be a sector to watch out for. National parks provide facilities for trekking, camping, wildlife viewing, and much more, whilst mountain areas provide an ideal opportunity for hill walking during the summer or skiing in winter.

Beautiful Bulgaria Project

The Bulgarian government has initiated a project called the *Beautiful Bulgarian Project* which aims to revitalise the tourist resorts and the historical architecture in the country. The majority of the financing for this project comes from the European Union, where it is estimated that over 4.5 million euros have been donated. This project also provides jobs for a number of previously unemployed individuals, providing vocational training etc. The project itself was initiated in 1997, and is currently in its third phase. The third phase is focussing on renovating some 200 tourist locations.

WINE

As one of the world's largest wine producers, Bulgaria boasts five wine-growing regions. In general, southern Bulgaria is known for its red wines, whilst northern Bulgaria for its white wines.

When we think of the great wine regions of the world, how many of us would instantly think of Bulgaria? It may surprise you to learn that in competitions between 2001 and 2003, some of Bulgaria's wines won five gold and 20 silver medals!

Summary of Bulgarian wines:

Wine	Description
Melnik	This grows in a small region of south west Bulgaria – famous for one of its customers – none other than Winston Churchill, former Prime Minister of England.
Mavrud	This has been around for over 1,000 years and is unique to Bulgaria.
Rubin	Known for its strong fruity bouquet and full red colour this wine is a cross between French Syrah and the Italian Nebbiolo.
Misket	Used for white wines such as Sungurlarski Misket and Vrachanski Misket. Grown in southern Bulgaria.
Dimiat	Known for its yellow colour and slight green tinge; this wine was brought to Bulgaria by the Phoenicians.
Pamid	This grape is used for light, red wines.

Red wines tend to be the dominant wine in Bulgaria. This is highlighted by the dominance of folklore songs about red wine. White wine, however, only features in one traditional folklore song, which includes the lyrics: 'O, white wine, why are you not red?'

♦ TOP TIP ♦

Check out the following website for more information about Bulgarian wines – http://bulgarianwines.com

EUROPEAN UNION

The Bulgarian currency, the Leva, was pegged to the euro in 2002 – with 1 euro equivalent to 1.95583 Leva.

Bulgaria was welcomed into the European Union on January 1st 2007, with a big New Year celebration in its capital city, Sofia. It is reported that Bulgaria's president, Georgi Parvanov, said that it was 'among the most important dates in Bulgaria's history'.

The addition of Bulgaria and Romania to the EU in 2007 enlarges the Union by another 29 million people, with each country having a GDP per capita of approximately one third of the EU average.

On 2 April 2004, there was an official ceremony at the NATO headquarters in Brussels marking the accession of Bulgaria, Estonia, Latvia, Lithuania, Slovakia, Slovenia and Romania to the North Atlantic Treaty Organisation.

INVESTMENT POTENTIAL

I will not be the first to tell you that no one can really predict the future, and when it comes to investment there are many factors that influence the success or failure of an opportunity.

Clearly, to invest in any country, one would hope for a stable economy and a government that is not likely to be ousted by a violent rebel group within a matter of days of being elected.

Whilst Bulgaria has had a turbulent past, it has been a democratic republic since 1990. Therefore, now in its second decade of democracy since leaving communism behind, it has started to mature and develop its infrastructure.

With funding from the EU, Bulgaria is well set to develop further over the next few years, building a strong foundation for the influx of foreign investment. Looking at the stock markets across the world, in 2003

Bulgaria beat them all in terms of percentage improvement – ranking a huge 160 per cent, compared to just 16 per cent in the United Kingdom. Speculation is also rampant on the subject of low-cost flights to the Black Sea Coast – usually a clear sign of ensuing economic prosperity related to an increase in tourism.

Some other reasons why Bulgaria should be considered for its investment potential are listed here:

- Among the lowest costs of doing business in Europe
- Robust legal framework focused on attracting and protecting foreign investment
- Fast improving business climate
  - among the lowest taxes in Europe
  - significant reduction in regulatory obstacles and start-up costs
- Institutional support for major foreign investment projects
- Modern telecom infrastructure, three mobile phone operators
- Superb academic and vocational training
- Excellent labour quality / labour cost ratio

BULGARIA IN THE MEDIA

You may no doubt be aware of the exposure of Bulgaria in a number of British television programmes over the last four years. Bulgaria has featured on the popular 'A Place In The Sun' programme on Channel 4 as well as ITV's 'I Want That House'.

Channel 4's 'A Place In The Sun' has featured the historic city of Veliko Turnovo; whilst ITV's 'I Want That House' featured the city of Ruse in North Bulgaria – Bulgaria's fifth largest city with a population of some 200,000.

Bulgaria has also featured in both property investment and other property related magazines – including the *Homes Overseas* magazine. In its October 2003 edition, Bulgaria featured number four in the top ten emerging markets – whilst in its September 2004 edition, Veliko Turnovo [Bulgaria] was voted as one of the locations in the top ten rural properties.

Quest Bulgaria magazine, produced in Sofia, reported in January 2007 that Bulgaria remains one of the favourite locations for homebuyers, together with Romania, Hungary and the Czech republic. Over 300,000 Brits now own a second home overseas with a prediction that 1.3 million British nationals could be living overseas by 2025!

MAGAZINES ON BULGARIA

To find out more about Bulgaria on a regular basis, there are two magazines that I would recommend. These magazines will allow you to keep up to date with the goings on in Bulgaria, the real estate market and much more.

Quest Bulgaria

Quest Bulgaria is a monthly magazine aimed at all those who are interested in Bulgaria, Bulgarian life and the real estate market in Bulgaria. The magazine is available by subscription to anywhere in the world. Anyone interested in subscribing can visit their web site at **www.questbulgaria.com** and get a free copy of the magazine sent to them first before subscribing.

As part of the subscription, readers also automatically become part of a loyalty discount scheme, offering discounts on services and products in Bulgaria, plus they get their own personal password to the Quest Bulgaria Ask the Expert discussion board where they can put their own questions to practicing experts (lawyers, accountants, etc) plus join in conversations with others who have moved to Bulgaria or have holiday homes in Bulgaria.

Vagabond

Vagabond delivers expert advice on investment and Bulgaria's booming real estate market, profiles of Bulgaria's business leaders and interviews with major players in the business world.

The magazine is a faithful friend to Bulgaria's ever-growing community of long-term foreign residents with insights into current affairs, politics and social issues, as well as interviews with the movers and shakers in business, politics, entertainment and culture, and features on the latest fashion, gadgets, books, films and music.

It is a helpful guide to visitors - providing all they need to know about where to eat, drink, sleep, see and be seen, with reviews and features on Bulgaria's choicest restaurants, bars, clubs and travel destinations. For more details about subscription visit their website at **www.vagabond-bg.com**.

TOO GOOD TO BE TRUE?

I know what you're thinking. It all sounds too good to be true doesn't it? Surely there are drawbacks, problems, other factors to consider? Yes, of course there are. So far we have looked at some of the positive factors that you should consider, if you are interested to buy property in Bulgaria. If you are looking to move to Bulgaria either to live, work, or retire, you do have to look at important issues such as language, health services, dealing with government officials and other institutions.

For a start, most form filling in Bulgaria is in the Bulgarian language – which is based on Cyrillic text. So, unless you are prepared to become fluent in Bulgarian, marry a Bulgarian or hire the services of a translator, you will face some practical difficulties here. That's not to say that these difficulties cannot be overcome. It just requires extra effort and may not suit everyone. English itself is spoken more amongst the younger generation, with more of the older generation being familiar with Russian and French.

Foreign Direct Investment in Bulgaria (by countries/years in EUR million)

No	Country	2000	2001	2002	2003	2004	2005	2006*
1	Austria	78.2	104.6	166.4	210.9	691.1	992.3	461.5
2	Belgium and Luxembourg	113.5	67.9	0.2	27.8	142.4	48.4	131.3
3	Cyprus	81.7	19.8	-8.4	104.9	90.1	6.1	105.3
4	Czech Republic	0.7	2.9	68.9	-6.1	279.5	118.3	208.9
5	Denmark	2.3	-0.6	4.2	43.4	13.4	19.2	74.8
6	France	41.7	16.5	8.9	20.5	51.1	27.4	66.1
7	Germany	42.3	75.3	90.8	96.1	253.0	68.2	138.6
8	Greece	105.8	262.3	240.1	198.9	179.6	286.1	283.1
9	Hungary	2.3	1.1	10.2	324.8	48.9	69.2	244.3
10	Ireland	3.6	-6.3	-1.8	2.6	19.7	85.8	253.1
11	Israel	9.1	0.1	3.3	4.8	12.7	9.6	40.5
12	Italy	379.5	163.9	25.1	87.8	71.2	108.4	63.4
13	Japan	1.8	3.5	14.3	0.6	4.0	20.9	43.9
14	Liechtenstein	4.3	7.6	6.8	11.3	14.6	3.4	2.1
15	Malta	1.0	3.0	1.1	7.4	3.1	4.5	6.7
16	Netherlands	-11.2	90.3	36.5	216.6	324.6	158.7	678.1
17	North Korea	0.0	0.0	0.0	0.0			0.1
18	Russia	25.0	-4.9	5.2	27.6	-15.9	86.2	79.5
19	South Korea	3.9	-10.2	0.4	-0.1	6.0	2.4	0.4
20	Spain	1.1	5.7	0.1	4.0	8.2	43.2	178.8
21	Sweden	2.5	6.3	30.7	6.1	15.2	12.0	16.9
22	Switzerland	27.2	37.0	39.3	134.2	116.5	249.1	26.3
23	Turkey	26.2	-10.8	16.4	-4.6	50.6	37.1	45.2
24	United Kingdom	-4.8	23.5	0.7	86.5	51.3	330.0	735.9
25	USA	61.8	49.9	60.0	112.8	107.7	53.5	116.0
26	Other	103.5	-4.9	160.6	131.6	197.5	262.2	363.1
	Total	**1103.3**	**903.4**	**980.0**	**1850.5**	**2735.9**	**3103.3**	**4364.0**

Source: Bulgarian Central Bank (* = preliminary data)

2

Visiting Bulgaria for the first time

If you are travelling from England then flights to Sofia run daily from London Gatwick. For example, you can depart by 10:30am and arrive in Sofia by 3:35pm (local time) with Bulgaria Air. With a flying time of some three hours, Bulgaria is easily accessible, and by early evening you can be dining in one of Sofia's finest.

VISA REQUIREMENTS

Since the first edition of this book the visa requirements have changed quite significantly. Due to the fact that rules and regulations do change in Bulgaria, it is important that you reference the latest information. You can reference the visa requirements on the Bulgarian embassy's website (www.bulgarianembassy.org.uk).

Effective from 1st January 2006, all children entering Bulgaria must have their own passport. Children included in their parents' passports will only be allowed entry if the passport also contains their photograph.

From 2007, the visa entry requirements are:

'I. Holders of valid ordinary passports from the following countries do not need a visa for a visit to Bulgaria for a period of up to 90 days within each period of six months:

Andora, Australia, Austria, Belgium, Brazil, Brunei, Canada, Chile, Costa Rica, Croatia, Cyprus, Czech Republic, Denmark, El Salvador, Estonia, Finland, France, Germany, Greece, Guatemala, Honduras, Hungary, Iceland, Ireland, Israel, Italy, Japan, Latvia, Liechtenstein, Lithuania, Luxembourg, Malta, Malaysia, Mexico, Monaco, Netherlands, New Zealand, Nicaragua, Norway, Panama, Paraguay, Poland, Portugal, Republic of Korea, Romania, San Marino, Singapore, Slovak Republic, Slovenia, Spain, Sweden, Switzerland, UK (British Citizen Passport Holders and British Nationals /Overseas/ only), USA, Uruguay, the Vatican, Venezuela, SAR – China (Hong Kong, Makao).

II. All holders of passports from countries not mentioned in the List above, need visas to enter Bulgaria.

POLICE REGISTRATION

If you enter Bulgaria as a non-EU/EEA citizen you must complete a registration form stating the address of where you will be staying and the purpose of your visit within five days of arrival. If you are staying in a hotel or guest accommodation, then this is generally handled for you. So if you are feeling a little uncomfortable about leaving your passports with the reception desk – don't worry, this is normal, and it's simply to take the burden away from you.

Having joined the European Union in 2007; if you enter Bulgaria as an EU citizen or a citizen of one of the EEA (Economic European Area) countries you no longer have to register with the police.

SAVING ON TELEPHONE / MOBILE COSTS IN BULGARIA

If you are visiting Bulgaria for the first time, you will probably want to avoid expensive phone calls incurred by using your own mobile's roaming service. The best way to handle this is to buy a pay-as-you-go type SIM card from one of the mobile providers in Bulgaria. The main operators are MTel, Vivatel and GloBul. You would typically pay 20 or 25 Leva for the start-up package, and then buy top-up cards that start from 15 Leva.

As you travel around Bulgaria and need to keep in touch with estate agents over the course of your trip, this makes for a much less expensive bill, and allows you to budget much better. This is assuming that you are mainly using the Bulgarian SIM card for calling other mobile users in Bulgaria. If, instead, you intend to call mainly landlines in Bulgaria, you can purchase a phonecard for the street phones. You can pick up a phonecard from as little as 2.50 Leva – and whilst they don't last forever, as long as you are calling landlines within Bulgaria, they certainly seem to!

How many of you have returned home from travels to find a huge mobile bill waiting for you, just because you either didn't think about the cost or didn't really care at the time!

KEEPING TELEPHONE COSTS DOWN FOR YOUR FRIENDS AND FAMILY

If you are planning to be in Bulgaria for more than a week or two, you may want family and friends to be able to get in touch with you. Or, you may be out on your own, and wanting your spouse to call you at the end of each day so that they can hear about the fabulous property bargains you have found! Clearly, calling Bulgaria from overseas can be a costly expense. However, there are numerous services available in many countries that allow you to substantially reduce your phone calls overseas.

In the UK, for example, there is a service provided by '18866' that provides very low-cost calls to Bulgaria. Calls to landlines are currently priced at 3p per minute, and calls to mobiles are currently priced at 20p per minute[3].

Wherever you are calling from, it is well worth researching a selection of communication companies who could help you to save on costs.

---

[3] These prices are subject to change and you should check with '18866' for the latest prices.

BOOKING ACCOMMODATION

It's a good idea to book your accommodation in advance if you are coming to Bulgaria for the first time. There are many internet sites advertising hotels and the majority provide photographs and details of the facilities. For convenience you may want to consider using a website that allows you to book over the internet. Alternatively you could follow the recommendations provided in travel guides to Bulgaria, such as '*Lonely Planet*'.

Like other parts of Eastern Europe, it is common to rent private apartments as an alternative to hotels or guest houses. This can generally save on costs and provide a larger living area and self-catering facilities etc. Such private apartments or villa's can be found easily on the internet.

I have provided some websites in Appendix H to assist you with your search for accommodation in Bulgaria.

Despite joining the EU in 2007 and the dual pricing of hotel accomodation in the country being outlawed; you can still find some hotels that practice a two-tier pricing structure. In this event, the price for local residents will be typically in Leva and the price for foreigners in euros. If you find yourself a victim, report them to the authorities!

WHAT MONEY SHOULD YOU CARRY?

After passing through the customs area at Sofia's international airport you may be greatly tempted to exchange some currency. Be warned though. Exchange rates are allegedly more expensive than can be found elsewhere and it would be better to exchange just enough for your taxi fare and to go to one of the banks in the city instead.

Now let's take a closer look in your wallet ... you've probably got a credit card or two sitting in there – and you're thinking to yourself, no problem, who needs cash? Credit cards are currently still not as widely accepted in Bulgaria as in other parts of Europe and whilst most of the larger hotels will accept your card, they may also add a surcharge of anything up to

4 per cent. That said, you should be able to use your credit card in some of the more established restaurants, shops etc. – but do be prepared to carry some cash.

IS AN ADAPTOR NEEDED FOR ELECTRICAL APPLIANCES?

Are you planning to take out any electrical appliances? If you're travelling from the UK, do purchase some European-style plug adaptors, since Bulgaria uses the two-pin plugs that are found in many other parts of Europe. This is especially important if you are bringing your hairdryer, mobile phone charger etc. Bulgaria's electricity supply runs on 220V with a frequency of 50Hz AC, and generally supports appliances configured for 240V.

GETTING AROUND

You may want to consider hiring a car, which you can book at the airport. Alternatively you can check out a series of internet-based sites where you can book online (see Appendix H for more details).

With taxis, you will find that rates vary, with prices starting from as little as 40–45 stotinki per kilometre (100 stotinki = 1 Leva). However, if you are not careful, you could find yourself paying almost double that (95 stotinki per km). It's best to look at the rates published on the taxi's window (usually on the front passenger side). Also, try to negotiate the rate before you start the journey if you don't feel comfortable with the meter. In some parts, taxi drivers are unscrupulous and have a button that they press to inflate the cost of the journey – usually evident when you are stopped at traffic lights and wondering why the meter is going wild. Do not accept this! If travelling in a major city, such as Sofia or Varna, an average fare within the city would typically range from between 2–5 Leva. Bulgaria travel guides will provide more information about recommended taxi pick-up points.

ACCESS TO THE INTERNET

If it's your first visit to the country and you know little about it, you may be forgiven for thinking that Bulgaria is in the dark ages when it comes to technology. However the internet, for example, is widely available – even in the most unlikely places! You can find an abundance of internet cafes in the cities where half an hour's internet usage can be from as little as 50 stotinki (18p sterling).

Why would you want internet access if you are out buying property you may ask? Well, a few reasons I would suggest are:

1. To research any local estate agents that you come across

2. To research properties available in Bulgaria on the internet

3. To check fluctuations in currency, if you are planning to buy soon

4. To check your email account (e.g. hotmail, yahoo etc.)

The connection speed in internet cafes is generally not that good (at least if you compare it to other parts of Western Europe) but it is functional and in the absence of choice, you have to take what you can get I'm afraid!

OPENING A BANK ACCOUNT

If you are seriously intending to buy property in Bulgaria, it's a good idea to open a bank account early on in your visit. This can save you some valuable time, particularly when you have lots of legal matters to attend to during the purchase.

I have found the quality of service offered by banks in Bulgaria varies quite a lot, as do their fee structures. I would recommend that you look for a bank that can offer you:

◆ Full internet banking (preferably with no monthly costs)

◆ Low fees (or no fees) for the receipt of foreign currency by electronic transfer

- A current account, that preferably pays interest[4]

- No monthly costs for holding the account

- Low (or no) initial deposit for opening the account

- English speaking tellers / representatives in the bank itself

- Low fees (or no fees) for withdrawing your own money!

Having lived and worked in Malaysia for several years, there were constant jokes about neighbouring Singapore. The most memorable one being how Malaysians would say that 'Singapore is a **fine** place to live'. They were, of course, referring to Singapore's strict regime of imposing fines on almost anything, anywhere at anytime. When it comes to banks in Bulgaria, I am reminded of this practice. Banks in Bulgaria do operate quite differently from many in Western Europe.

One of the hardest things to come to terms with is that they seem to charge you for practically anything you want to do, and seem to miss the point that you are leaving your money with them (which they subsequently invest / loan to others). This is not uncommon in Eastern Europe. I have seen similar practices in Estonia, where they also charge you a monthly fee for having a bank account, and have similar fee structures. Believe it or not, many will also charge you for withdrawing money from your bank account. This can be based on either a percentage (e.g. 0.01%) or based on a fixed cost per withdrawal (e.g. 1 euro per withdrawal). And yes, this even applies to withdrawing the money in cash from the branch itself!

You shouldn't expect the bank to explain all these terms and conditions to you. I was once charged over 150 euros for just withdrawing my own money in cash from a bank in Bulgaria. The receipt from the transaction did not show this charge and it was only later whilst reviewing a statement that it was found. Be careful.

---

[4] Any interest paid is better than none!

To make matters worse, when you transfer money from your country to Bulgaria, some banks often charge you for the receipt of that money in your Bulgarian bank account. Now, whilst the majority of us are used to flat fees for bank transfers, in Bulgaria some of the banks charge you a **percentage** of the amount you are receiving. That is, they do not charge you a fixed fee. So, if you are transferring quite a large sum for the final payment on your property, some banks may quite happily take a percentage of that from you. I bet you didn't factor that into your purchase costs?

I also bet that the agent you used didn't tell you about the potential bank charges either! This will change, in time, especially after those of you reading this book have told them!

You will find it very difficult to find a bank that meets all the criteria above, but I can tell you that it's possible to find banks that meet a good majority of them.

It is worth shopping around for the best bank to suit your needs – others you may want to review include CB Allianz Bulgaria, (bank.allianz.bg), Bulbank (www.bulbank.bg), Postbank (www.postbank.bg) and First Investment Bank (www.fibank.bg).

◆ TOP TIP ◆

To avoid being charged for withdrawing cash when you plan to pay a deposit or final payment, set up a bank transfer to the seller instead, which will save you money. Bank transfers tend to have low, fixed fees.

3

Location, location, location

You have probably heard a thousand times the phrase 'location, location, location'. This is a key point as you contemplate the choice of property. It's important that the property you buy will appeal to others, particularly if you intend to resell it in the future or rent it out.

So what kind of factors should you consider about the location?

BASIC CHECKS ABOUT THE LOCATION

You must check is that the location of your property or plot of land has all the services that you require.

This includes:

1. Electricity

2. Water

3. Communications (i.e. telephone line)

4. Access to cable TV [if this is important to you]

5. Canalisation or septic tanks for sewage treatment

In Bulgaria, it is still not uncommon to find areas even within a few kilometres of a major city that do not have some of the basic facilities that the rest of Western Europe (for example) take for granted. When you are buying a property (or a plot of land) you should always ensure that you ask these questions and if possible insist on this being clarified in the preliminary contract as a condition of the sale. Your solicitor can then check that the property / plot has the services either on the plot or nearby.

Usually the estate agents will tell you what services are available. Sometimes they will tell you that one or more of the services are 'nearby'. Do make sure that you ask for clarification of what 'nearby' means. Does it mean within one metre or within two hundred metres, for example? If there is no water on the plot, or nearby, then it's typical in some areas to dig a well. So if there is no water, ask the agent whether it's possible to dig a well to provide a water supply. If it is, then you will have free water!

If it's important to you to have access to cable TV then do ask whether the specific area is able to gain access to the cable. Sometimes it's helpful to ask the neighbours when you are looking around the plots. If you don't speak Bulgarian then you can always consider asking your estate agent to translate for you or alternatively look at hiring the services of a local translator. It is also possible to install a satellite dish, so if your property is not located in a convenient area for cable TV, then this should not put you off! Please see p.92 for more information about the options for installing satellite TV.

CHECKS TO MAKE IF YOU ARE PLANNING TO LIVE / RETIRE IN BULGARIA

If you are planning to live or retire in Bulgaria, then you need to think more about day-to-day practicalities and how well the location caters to these. For example:

1. Is the property situated on a convenient public transport route (and how often do the buses run)?

2. Are there any local shops?

3. Are there schools nearby (if you have children)?

4. Are there international schools (where English is the preferred language)?

5. Is the property in an attractive location?

6. Is it within easy reach of the town/city centre?

7. What are the roads like in winter (i.e. are they still accessible)?

8. If on the Black Sea Coast, how far is the nearest beach?

9. Are there other foreigners in the area (which may be either a good or a bad thing!)?

10. What are the likely noise levels of the location (if you are specifically looking for a quiet location, for example)?

11. Is the property in a landslide area [or so called 'red zone']?

CHECKS TO MAKE IF YOU ARE INVESTING IN BULGARIA

If you are investing, you may want to focus more on the 'cosmetic' appeal of the property and its location, for example:

1. If the property is on the Black Sea Coast is it close to the beach?

2. Does it have beautiful views over the countryside or sea?

3. Is it within easy reach of café's and restaurants?

4. Are there plenty of activities nearby?

5. Is it photogenic?

6. What are the other properties like in the area?

7. Does the property have a swimming pool or access to a pool in the local area?

8. How have the property / land prices done over the last three to five years in this area?

9. What are the rental yields like in this area (or what are they likely to be if not yet established)?

10. Is the property on a bus route or an easily accessible location by other means of public transport?

As an investor, you are likely to be looking for either a rental income from your property or capital gains on the eventual resale. It is therefore important to focus on the 'cosmetic' appeal of your property and its location. Ask the kind of questions that your potential tenant / buyer would ask and ensure that it meets these criteria.

CHECKS TO MAKE IF YOU ARE BUYING OFF-PLAN

Buying off-plan is the process of reserving a property on a new development before the property is completed. In many cases, the actual construction may not have even started when you put your deposit down on the property. You would generally review a floor plan of the property and also an artist's impression of the final property exterior.

When buying off-plan, the payments would normally be profiled during the stages of construction, typically with an initial reservation fee followed by two or three more payments spread out over the construction cycle.

As you drive through Bulgaria you will see examples of building projects that have never been completed. Whilst this is less common now, you should always check the credentials of the building company to ensure that they have a good track record and also conduct as many checks on the developer / investor as you can.

Off-plan developments are particularly common in Bulgaria, with projects running in major cities and ski-resorts; for example in Sofia, Varna, Sunny Beach and Bansko. Sunny Beach has been a particular favourite amongst the British!

If you are buying off-plan, do ensure that you have viewed the final site development plan and understand what amenities, if any, will be provided. It is also advisable, if you have the time (and money), to visit the site of the proposed development to ensure that you are happy with the location. No matter how many questions you ask about the location, or how many two-dimensional photographs you see, nothing can really compare to seeing it with your own eyes. If you are buying off-plan with a view to living there, this is even more important.

4

How to buy property in Bulgaria

Whether you have already made a decision to buy a home in Bulgaria, or you are contemplating the idea, you must start to familiarise yourself with the whole buying process. In this chapter we shall look at the buying process in some detail to try to remove all your fears and equip you with the information you need to be able to make a successful purchase.

With price increases in real estate reaching double digits between 2002 and 2003, real estate growth is expected to continue. In the last quarter of 2003, you could expect to pay, on average, 450-500 euros per square metre for a new build. By the first quarter of 2004 this had already risen to between 600-650 euros per square metre – with prices peaking at 800–1,000 euros per square metre at the top end, for the more luxurious villa's and apartments. In 2008, one of the most expensive districts in Sofia, Doctors Garden, you can expect to pay in excess of 2000 euros per square metre for a fully furnished two bedroom apartment in the capital city.

Over the next few sections we will look in more detail at the steps that you should follow when buying a property in Bulgaria, which can be summarised simply in the following ten steps.

THE TEN BASIC STEPS TO BUYING PROPERTY IN BULGARIA

1. Research before you buy!

2. Find your home

3. Negotiate the price

4. Make an offer

5. Set up a Bulgarian company if the property has land

6. Ask your solicitor to conduct all legal checks, debts on the property etc.

7. Sign a preliminary contract and pay the deposit

8. Sign the notary deed (i.e. the final contract upon which you take ownership)

9. Make the final payment (typically immediately after signing the notary deed)

10. Pat yourself on the back and celebrate!

Whilst these steps provide a simple view of the whole buying process, those of you who have dealt with estate agents before will probably be questioning the sequence of steps 6 and 7. Shouldn't they be the other way around?

Well, strictly speaking – no – you should allow your solicitor to conduct the basic checks prior to signing the preliminary contract. You may find yourself being pressured to jump almost immediately into signing the preliminary contract though. Try to avoid this, and get the basic checks done. We will cover this in more detail when we explore the joys of dealing with estate agents and solicitors later in the chapter.

Clearly, this is an over-simplified view, but if you take it in stages and focus on each stage at a time, it should be no less stressful than buying a home anywhere else in the world.

RESEARCH BEFORE YOU BUY

It never ceases to amaze me at the growing number of people who are buying property in Bulgaria, but are oblivious to the local geography or indeed the whole process of buying a home in Bulgaria.

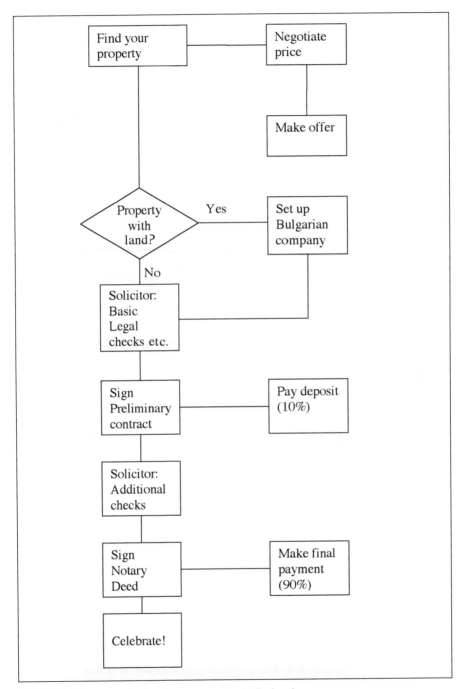

FIGURE 1 The steps for buying a property in Bulgaria

As with any investment, you should not enter into it lightly, and spend some time investigating the market. Read as many articles as you can about real estate investment (particularly those that focus on Eastern Europe). Also, I would recommend that you visit as many property investment seminars as you can to understand what it's all about. Even if your purchase is a home, rather than an investment, you need to understand how you may be affected in the future.

There are only a limited number of books on Bulgaria, but I would suggest you read whatever you can find about the geography – and travel guides are a great source of information. You may also subscribe to a number of property magazines such as *Homes Overseas* and *Property Investor*, both of which regularly look at properties in Eastern Europe. For more information on the many locations within Bulgaria, I would recommend the *Lonely Planet guide to Bulgaria*, by Paul Greenway. This is an excellent source of information and would allow you to study the geography in more detail.

One of the most obvious and perhaps most convenient sources of information on Bulgaria is the internet. If you can get access to the internet, you will find a wealth of information and forums where you can ask questions to others who have bought property in Bulgaria. I have personally found the internet-based forums a valuable source of information and have met some very welcoming and helpful people in this way.

FINDING YOUR PROPERTY

There are numerous ways of searching for your property – with perhaps one of the most convenient being to use the internet. With many estate agents offering properties for sale on the internet, it's not difficult to see why this method would be so appealing. But there are drawbacks.

Perhaps one of the biggest drawbacks is the fact that many of the properties that you are viewing and setting your heart on, have, in fact, already been sold! Naturally, some sites are better than others, but I would advise you not to be solely reliant on the internet. I have heard stories about people who have bought properties based only on what they have seen on the internet. This is certainly not advisable, and I would urge you all to take the time to visit any property you are considering to buy. By all means use the internet for research, but take my advice and do not make your purchase decisions until you have actually seen the property with your own eyes!

You might be surprised to learn that a growing number of people are buying properties in Bulgaria, over the internet, with the same ease with which they would purchase a book on Amazon! At least with Amazon you have the option to read independent reviews on the book you are buying! Buying property over the internet without viewing it could be argued to be a foolish and irresponsible approach to investment and one that could inherit a multitude of problems.

So, how else can you find your ideal home? There are several ways that you can go about it, depending on your budget, your nervous system and your sense of adventure! Let's look at the different approaches you could take.

◆ TOP TIP ◆

Use the PropertyDragon website (www.propertydragon.com) to view the varied properties and land plots vailable in Bulgaria. It has a very easy to use search engine, where you can choose Bulgaria as the country. You can then view the real estate offers available from many estate agents and private sellers, and contact the owners or agents directly, after you have registered on the site.

Viewing trips

A good starting point, having decided on the type of property and / or location you want, is to take a viewing trip of properties in Bulgaria.

Viewing trips typically last two or three days (but could be longer!) and allow you to visit a good cross section of properties that meet your criteria. When you are unfamiliar with a particular location, viewing trips are certainly a good introduction and there are a few companies based in the UK that can provide such trips to Bulgaria.

Viewing trips to Bulgaria, like viewing trips to other countries, have a fee associated with them. As each company works slightly differently, you need to be comfortable with their fee structure. At the time of writing, you should expect to pay approximately 75 euros a day to view properties from a UK-based agent – adding to that the cost of your flight and accommodation in Bulgaria.

Alternatively, you could contact one of the Bulgarian agents and organise your own viewing trip – providing your criteria to them by email / telephone and request that they make an itinerary for your viewing trip. They would also be able to assist in arranging your accommodation and flights, if necessary. With a local Bulgarian agent, viewing properties may only involve the cost of petrol for showing you around the properties over your two to three day trip (for example, 20 Leva a day). But some of the agents do not charge you anything for viewing properties.

Please see Appendix H for a list of both local Bulgarian estate agents and UK- based agents.

Preparing for your viewing trip

Prior to your viewing trip I would recommend that you clearly define the criteria of the property (or properties if you are feeling ambitious!) that you are looking for. You can then send these criteria to either the UK-based agent or the local Bulgarian agent that you intend to use during your trip.

Decide on the features that the property **must have**. For example, you may list:

1. Villa of approximately €100,000 budget

2. Good investment potential for capital growth

3. Located in Varna, Balchik or near Golden Sands

4. Excellent sea view

5. Minimum three bedrooms

6. Photogenic (may be important if you are renting it out)

7. Must appeal to Western holidaymakers

8. Must have a heating system in working order

9. Must have indoor toilets

10. Must have a shower in the main bathroom

Then make a list of features that would be **nice to have**, but not essential. For example:

1. Walking distance to the beach

2. On a quiet street

3. On a street with a pavement (many houses, particularly in some villages, do not have developed roads or pavements)

4. Has a traditional Bulgarian fireplace

5. Includes all furniture in the price

6. Has terrace area or balcony

7. Has a garden

8. On a street with other nice / developed houses

9. A traditional Bulgarian style house (with the stone and wood design)

Following this organised approach before your trip, will not only help you to concentrate on properties that fall in the category that you want, but they also help the agent to focus their efforts on what you are looking for and plan a viewing trip that is less likely to disappoint you.

It is also a good idea to do your homework on the particular regions you are considering. Talk to the agent about the different regions and see what they advise, but also take the time to research the country.

In order to assist you, take a look at the rough guide below:

What you are looking for	Possible locations to consider
Property close to the sea, beach or with sea views	Somewhere along the Black Sea Coast; possibly considering areas close to major cities such as Varna and Burgas
A place with natural historic interest	Veliko Turnovo Plovdiv Vidin Koprivshtitsa Ruse (North Bulgaria)
A bustling city life, with lots of activities, past-times	Sofia (the capital) Plovdiv Varna
A place to retire, with beautiful scenery, quiet area, with other foreign families in the area	Rogachevo (7 km to Albena resort) Tsurkva (5 km to Albena resort) Balchik Arbanassi Veliko Turnovo [The list is endless, but these are a few of my favourites]
All year round rental potential	Sofia Varna
A tourist resort location, with lots of night-life and activities	Golden Sands (near Varna) Sunny Beach (near Burgas) Albena (30 km from Varna)
A quieter resort (out of season)	Sveti Vlas (near Burgas) Ravda village (near Burgas)
A picturesque town, close to the sea	Sozopol (near Burgas) Nessebar Sinemorets
Within 15-30 minutes of an international airport	Sofia Varna Burgas
Close to the mountains – e.g. for skiing etc.	Sofia (Vitosha Mountain) Rila (Rila Mountains) Pamporovo (Rodopi Mountains) Melnik (Pirin Mountains) Borovets (Pirin Mountains) Bansko (Pirin Mountains) Dobrinishte (Pirin Mountains)
Current areas of interest amongst investors	Sunny Beach Varna Burgas Pamporovo Bansko Veliko Turnovo
Pretty village, cobblestone streets	Tryavna

Planning

Before you visit Bulgaria to start the whole process of buying your property, you should seriously think about the people that you will need to assist you through the whole process.

These include:

◆ Solicitor (you will probably need a local Bulgarian solicitor)

◆ Estate agent (this may be a UK-based company or a local Bulgarian one)

◆ Accountant (you may want to seek independent tax advice both in your country of residence and from a Bulgarian accountant)

◆ Translator (you can find local Bulgarian translators or ask the estate agent to recommend one for you)

You may use the solicitor recommended by your agent, who typically works for the same company as your agent. However, you are best advised to use an independent solicitor who is more likely to work in your best interests, and not the interests of the company that they are working for!

Typical costs to consider

As part of your planning you should also consider all the costs that you are likely to incur as a result of buying property in Bulgaria. These include:

◆ Return airfare to Bulgaria

◆ Any agency fees (e.g. for UK-based agencies)

◆ Viewing trip fees (if you take this route)

◆ The cost of setting up a Bulgarian company (if the property has land)

◆ Legal fees (for solicitors and notary public)

◆ Accountancy fees (for any consultations with accountants)

◆ Accommodation costs in Bulgaria

- Taxes (government taxes and local court fees for notary deed)

- Estate agent/agency commissions

- Potential renovation costs (if you are buying an old or unfinished property)

- Translation fees (for the translation of legal documents into English)

- Transport costs (e.g. cost for domestic flights to the Black Sea Coast, bus fares, taxis)

So whilst you may be tempted to rip out your cheque book to pay the 7,000 euros for a country retreat in Bulgaria, do be clear that there are a number of costs associated with that purchase that mean the total cost of your purchase will be higher than the offer price for the property!

Using a UK-based agent

There are currently a small number of UK-based companies who provide a service to help you find property in Bulgaria. These tend to be small companies, some family based, who work together with Bulgarian partners to provide you with the full service – from taking your initial requirements, to organising your flights and hotel accommodation and guiding you through the whole process of buying a home in Bulgaria.

An obvious advantage of this approach is that you can deal with people within the UK, saving on expensive phone calls, and for some people this provides a more comfortable and familiar way of dealing with a property purchase overseas.

Costs for UK agents

Commission rates for UK-based companies do vary quite a lot – from as little as 2.5 per cent, rising to 10 per cent and above; whilst others include a fixed price for properties that cost up to a certain amount. Provided you understand what their services include and can justify the cost of these fees, then you could consider using one of these UK-based agents.

Do be sure to check if there are any additional costs. Like most things in life, if you don't read the small print, you may get disappointed when confronted with a bill you weren't expecting. So, do check if there are additional costs for:

1. The translation of legal documents

2. Payments to the notary when signing preliminary and final contracts

3. Payments to solicitors for their legal checks, preparing legal papers etc.

4. Payment of local and court taxes

5. Payment for the registration of the property with the local authorities

6. Payment for the set-up of a Bulgarian company (if required)

Basically, I would suggest insisting on **all** costs that you may incur being stated upfront. You can then budget your finances much more accurately, and avoid being irritated when another cost is sprung on you by surprise.

Should you use a UK-based agent?

On your first trip to Bulgaria it may be in your interests to go via one of the UK-based agents, in order to show you the ropes, as it were. If you are of a nervous disposition or would prefer less hassle, it may be in your interests to choose this route. It is wise to spend some time getting to know the agents, how they work and if possible contacting people that have bought from them, so that you know what to expect.

In my experience, I have heard both good and bad reports of UK-based agents. But the same is true of local Bulgarian estate agents. At the end of the day, you have to take the responsibility for the choices you make – and that means doing your homework.

But, if you are feeling more adventurous and would like to approach local estate agents instead, then read on …

Using a Bulgarian estate agent

Bulgaria enjoys a healthy number of estate agents, and to be fair, they tend to provide a good standard of service. It is a very competitive market though and you are almost spoilt for choice. Therefore, making the decision of which agent to use can be quite daunting.

Most important of all, be comfortable with the people you are dealing with. It will help you to find an estate agent with English speaking agents – but at the same time, you can also consider hiring the services of a local translator – where you can expect to pay around 20 Leva per hour.

I know what you are thinking – why don't I recommend an estate agent for you? Well, I would hardly be offering you an impartial view of buying a property in Bulgaria if I did that, would I? However, in order to help you to 'establish contacts' I have added many estate agents to Appendix H at the end of this book for your reference – both UK-based agents and local Bulgarian estate agents.

What I can say, though, is try to speak to other people who have either bought in Bulgaria or you know are planning to buy out there. There are very helpful internet-based forums which provide a wealth of experiences from many individuals who are both living and investing in Bulgaria (see Appendix H). Whilst you need to carefully consider taking any advice you receive on such forums, these are very helpful resources for meeting with others who have either already bought a property in Bulgaria or are contemplating it – a great opportunity to compare notes and learn the ropes.

Local agent fees

The majority of local estate agents do not charge any fee for viewing properties. However, it's best to check this before viewing the properties.

The more professional agents will generally ask you to fill in a form in which you agree to their terms and conditions, and they also have a tendency to list the properties that you are going to view on a particular day – and ask you to sign each one that you have seen at the end of the day.

As for commission, it's quite common for the local estate agents to request three per cent commission. This does, generally, include all of the required paperwork for the purchase and associated legal fees (if you see their solicitor). You can of course attempt to negotiate the fees, but will probably have more luck with the smaller agents. Do remember that you generally get what you pay for.

The solo approach

The slightly more adventurous amongst you may choose not to use either UK or local-based agents. I have heard of some cases where people follow this approach and with success. Your success relies on being able to communicate with the locals and perhaps talking to restaurant owners or town officials about what properties are available in the area.

You may also consider looking in local newspapers and working with a local translator, approaching vendors directly. This will save you the usual three per cent agency fees, but does mean that you are very much on your own, and is clearly a higher-risk strategy. But do be sure to hire the services of a good lawyer to conduct all the legal checks and produce the required documentation.

As I have mentioned throughout this book, the existence of several useful internet-based forums also offers other means – for example, hiring the services of a local person (by recommendation on the forum) to assist you in finding properties. You could typically expect to pay 30 Leva a day for local assistance.

This approach is obviously more time-consuming than the other options – for example, it may require anything from two to four weeks – because you will need to meet directly with the vendors and possibly arrange your own transport. Do take these factors into account.

You might laugh, but you will also hear stories of people who have used taxi drivers, also recommended on the forums, to assist in locating/buying homes in Bulgaria. Whatever approach you take, be sure to seek professional legal advice before you part with any of your money and if something sounds too good to be true it more than likely is!

How do I view the properties on offer?

You may notice a distinct shortage of 'FOR SALE' signs in Bulgaria. It is true to say that the real estate business does not operate in quite the same way as it does in England (for example).

There is very little difference in how you view properties in Bulgaria. If it's a new-build, then the agent will take you to see the property directly, key in hand. Don't be alarmed if you are ferried into a taxi – as this is not unusual. Some of the larger estate agents tend to have company cars to ferry you around.

Perhaps one difference you will notice is that the agents do also work together, and you may be introduced to another agent when you arrive at the property. Again, don't be alarmed as this is also quite normal. If you find that estate agents start to quietly discuss things in Bulgarian, don't panic. It can be a little intimidating if you don't speak the language but it is nothing to worry about.

What standards should I expect?

One term that you will hear quite a lot is that the building you are about to see is of 'Bulgarian standard'. What this generally means for a 'new-build' is that the interior is an empty shell, with no finished floors (i.e. just a concrete floor), an unfinished bathroom (i.e. no bath, toilet, shower etc.) and no kitchen furniture or appliances. It would also suggest, typically:

- PVC windows
- Internal doors installed, but not finished (i.e. may be in need of painting, and fixtures/fittings for door handles, lock etc.)
- No tiles (e.g. no bathroom or kitchen tiles on the floors or walls)
- Installation of the electricity cables, but no sockets installed
- Installation of the water supply, but no fittings to kitchen/bathroom etc.
- Smooth plastered walls and ceilings, but not painted
- Walls in place, dividing the rooms

For new-builds, it's not uncommon to buy apartments to this 'Bulgarian standard'. This is also referred to as the 'Bulgarian National Standard'.

So, is this a bad thing? Well, no, not really. In Bulgaria, the locals prefer to make the decisions on the finishing work for themselves, so this is actually the preferred way of purchasing a new home. It just means that you have to budget for the finishing work.

At this point, you may wish to follow a nagging instinct ... a voice in your head that's almost singing to you ... 'survey; got to get a survey ...'. Am I right?

GETTING A SURVEY

So, you're thinking, survey, and your thinking this has to be the next logical step? Wrong. Well, it's not wrong, it's just not that common in Bulgaria to get a survey done when buying a house. So when you ask the selling agent about getting a survey this may explain the dumbfounded looks that you get!

But all is not lost. You can either ask the agent to organise a survey for you or ask to speak to a local architect or building company and engage their services to look over the property for you. They could even produce a report for you. The best advice I can give you is to find someone independent to look over the property. Although I have yet to come across anyone in Bulgaria who is employed as a 'surveyor', many builders are willing to provide this service.

THE TWO-TIER PRICING STRUCTURE IN BULGARIA

You may have heard that there is a two-tier pricing structure for real estate in Bulgaria – which may be a concern to you.

With such a two-tier system still found for hotel accommodation in the country it is no wonder that some people assume that the prices are raised for foreign buyers.

It is easy to be sceptical when you consider that the average Bulgarian salary is 181 euros[6] a month. This equates to an annual salary of 2,172

---

[6] This figure was published by the National Statistics Institute, Bulgaria, in 2007.

euros. So, when you see properties selling for the equivalent of 35,000 euros and above, it is difficult to understand how the local residents are able to afford such properties. How many mortgage lenders in England do you know that will lend you 16 times your annual income?

During a seminar hosted by the British Bulgarian Chamber of Commerce in London, May 2004, this very question about the alleged two-tier pricing structure was put forward to the guest panellists – which included representatives from Bulgarian estate agents. Here, the notion of a dual price for real estate was categorically denied.

In my dealings with agents, both in the UK and Bulgaria, I have also asked this question many times, and am repeatedly told that such a system does not exist. There will, of course, be exceptions – and some sellers may naturally take advantage of foreign buyers as they would in other parts of the world. What is important, at the end of the day, is that you are comfortable with the price that you are going to pay for a property. If, after comparing the price of the property you are interested in with many others of a similar type, you feel that it is a fair price and good value for money – and it meets all your other criteria – then go for it!

If, on the other hand, you feel that the price on offer is just way over the mark, and no amount of negotiation is going to change that, then simply move on. With the increased interest in Bulgaria amongst foreign investors, there are more and more properties up for sale – and a good choice – so you are also in a strong position as a buyer.

NEGOTIATING THE PRICE

Before agreeing to purchase the property, it is always a good idea to negotiate the price, just as you would in many other countries in the world. If you are using an agent, then tell the agent what price you are prepared to pay for the property and the agent will then negotiate on your behalf (in theory). But do note that the agent is actually lowering their own commission by negotiating a lower price for you – which is not a good incentive for them to achieve the best possible price for you. They will of course tell you that they will get the best price for you, but what do you expect them to say! It is difficult, as it

HOW TO BUY PROPERTY IN BULGARIA / **43**

would not be appropriate for you to deal with the owner directly when going through an agent. What this means, realistically, is that you need to be prepared to walk away. Be firm, and have several properties lined up. You could also consider offering a bonus commission to the agent if they get the price you want. That way, there's an additional incentive for them.

But do your homework and have a good appreciation of the selling prices of the kind of properties you are interested in. Some unscrupulous agents may increase the price when they know a foreigner is buying; so be aware of this, and be prepared to negotiate. Many sellers in Bulgaria are prepared to sit on their property or land until the 'right' buyer comes along, so negotiation may not always work in your favour.

◆ TOP TIP ◆

My best advice to you is to view as many properties as you can in the time that you have and be prepared to put in offers for more properties than perhaps you intend to buy.

Based on my own experiences and experiences of others that I have met, if you just put in an offer for one property you may find that there is some legal issue with that property and, if so, have to start the whole viewing process again. It can also be quite demoralising at first if you are disappointed early in the process.

So let's say that you have made your offer. What's next?

SETTING UP A BULGARIAN COMPANY

The next stage is to determine whether the property that you want to buy has land associated with it or not. The reason being that if it has land, then you will have to form a company in order to purchase it.

'A company – I don't like the sound of that!', you may be thinking to yourself. Well, I can sympathise with this view, but there is nothing untoward about this procedure. In order to own land in Bulgaria, you either have to be Bulgarian or buy it under a Bulgarian registered company. This is because under the current legislation, Bulgarian law forbids foreign individuals from owning land.

At this point some of you may be tempted to walk away. However, it's really just a formality, and perfectly above the law, so what are you waiting for? If you really feel that there is something unlawful about this then contact your local Bulgarian embassy.

On the other hand, if you are buying an apartment, you can generally get away without forming a company. Apartment purchases are, therefore, comparatively more straightforward. But there are exceptions. If you are buying an apartment that has land associated with it, you will also need to form a Bulgarian company. So don't be fooled by those agents who may lead you to believe that you will not have to form a company if you are buying an apartment. There are exceptions.

If you are buying a typical new-build apartment that comes with an extra two or three metre square storage area, then you are virtually assured of a company-free purchase. Perhaps you always wanted to be your own boss anyway, and setting up a company comes to you naturally – or perhaps becoming the sole or joint directors of a company overnight appeals. Whatever your motivation, let me take you through the fairly simple process of setting up a Bulgarian company to allay your fears.

Whether you are working with a UK-based agent, or one of the local agents, setting up a company couldn't be easier. There are only three real decisions that you need to make:

1. What do you want to call your company?

2. Who are the directors (shareholders) of the company and what stake do they each have?

3. What registered office address do you want to use for the company?

Is that all there is to it? Well, pretty much – but here are a few more details about how your company gets formed.

Meeting with the agent to discuss the company formation

It all starts in a meeting that usually includes your local agent/representative, a translator and a solicitor. Of course, whether you appoint your own solicitor or use the one recommended by the agent, is your choice. Common advice would be to choose your own independent solicitor. It's all a question of what you are comfortable with at the end of the day. If you are prepared to trust your agent, then why not trust their recommended solicitor? It's not really my place to influence your decision – just be sure that you are comfortable either way.

What you will be told (usually prior to this meeting) is that you need to set up a company bank account, with an initial deposit of 3,500 Leva. In some cases, you will be told 5,000 Leva. In actual fact, the initial amount for the creation of the company can be as low as 3,500 Leva. So, what happens to this money? Well, it's ultimately destined to come back to you, after its short vacation in your newly set-up company bank account. So don't worry, it's not a fee.

Surely there are more costs? Well, yes, there is the fee for setting up the company itself – which involves various paperwork and court appearances. Thankfully, this can all be done by the appointed solicitor for you, provided you provide them with power of attorney.

There. I've said it. Those three little words that strike fear into every fibre of our being. Those three words that are responsible for more anxiety amongst foreign investors than any other three words ever uttered from time immemorial! POWER OF ATTORNEY. There, I've said it again, and I've capitalised it!

Power of attorney

So what is the big deal about power of attorney? Well, to be fair, some people have been burnt by unscrupulous traders who abuse this power to either take money or cheat them out of some land etc.

However, by applying a modicum of common sense, one can quite easily amend the terms of power of attorney contracts to your advantage. The addition of a few extra clauses can provide you with the 'eiderdown feather' comfort you require for those long nights ahead.

You set up power of attorney for a number of areas that need to be addressed. These are typically:

1. Power of attorney for the solicitor to set up the company on your behalf, deposit the initial monies into the company bank account and withdraw payments for the final contract.

2. Power of attorney for the agent (or solicitor) to withdraw the deposit for the property, to pay the owner.

3. Power of attorney to your husband/wife for your local bank account, as bank accounts in Bulgaria tend not to operate in 'joint' names.

◆ TOP TIP ◆

If you are uncomfortable with the idea of power of attorney, then you can introduce additional terms for your protection. I find generally that people are uncomfortable to give power of attorney control over their bank account.

In this case, you can apply a time period over which your solicitor or appointed agent has power of attorney and you can also limit the maximum amount for a withdrawal and even state the number of withdrawals you will allow – e.g. allow only one withdrawal of a fixed amount. This may typically cover either the initial deposit, and/or the final payment.

How long does it take to set up a company?

As for the fees associated with setting up a company, these vary considerably. It depends on how long you are prepared to wait for the company to be set-up. The average duration for the set up of a company is between 20 and 30 days. For this, you should not have to pay more than 600 euros in total.

If you don't have 20 to 30 days and need to act faster, some agents can offer a fast-track service. In this case expect to pay more. Anything up to 1,200 euros! Again, you get what you pay for. As long as you are comfortable, then don't worry. Compared to the amount you are investing in the property, this is peanuts!

What to expect when your company has been formed

Once your company has been formed, you should expect a few documents. These include:

◆ Tax registration, which takes the form of a plastic card, slightly larger than a credit card – this card is white and has an emblem containing two green lions

◆ BULSTAT card, which is a similar size to a credit card. Every company receives a BULSTAT number, equivalent to the company registration number

◆ Documents detailing the incorporation of the company

◆ A company stamp, required when stamping various documents on behalf of the company

As you will have most likely set up a limited liability company, your company name will have the suffix OOD – which is the Bulgarian equivalent of a limited liability company (i.e. 'Ltd' in the UK).

Having formed your company, negotiated the price and made a formal offer, you are now ready to sign the preliminary contract. In practice, it is also common to prepare the preliminary contract before the company has been formally registered. Of course, the final contract (notary deed) will clearly specify that the property is being purchased by the company (and its company representatives).

Signing the preliminary contract

The first contract that you will sign will be the preliminary contract. This will typically be drawn up in the Bulgarian language – in which case it is advisable to have a translator present to translate its contents to you verbally.

There are some companies who will provide the preliminary contract in English (together with the Bulgarian version), which makes the whole process much easier. Do note that the final contract (notary deed) must exist in the Bulgarian language to be legal. If you are asked to sign a final contract that is ONLY in English, this will not be legally binding in Bulgaria.

The preliminary contract itself is signed by both parties, i.e. you the buyer and the individual(s) selling the property. In this contract, you will generally find the full specification of what you are buying and any land associated with the property will be quoted in square metres. Do ensure that the amount of land quoted is what you were told by the estate agent/owner. The contract will state the actual deposit amount that you will give to the buyer and will contain any protective clauses added by your solicitor. Please refer to Appendix N to view a sample preliminary contract.

Paying the deposit

At the time of signing the preliminary contract you will also (generally) be expected to pay a 10 per cent deposit to the owner. This is generally expected to be paid in cash, and is handed to the owner after the contract has been signed by both parties. However, do not be afraid to request a bank transfer if you are uncomfortable making a cash deposit.

Now, you may be in the situation that you don't carry 6,000 euros for this occasion. So, it's not uncommon to agree a smaller amount to be handed over at the point of signing the contract – with an agreement to settle the remainder of the deposit within 7-10 days. For example, 1,000-2,000 euros is generally accepted at this stage. As a rule this is also added to the preliminary contract – so it is your legal duty to settle the deposit by the date stated.

At the point of signing the preliminary contract your solicitor will typically verfiy the identity of the buyer/seller by checking indentity cards and passports as applicable. Later on, when you sign the final contract (notary deed), the notary public will check the identity documents for the buyer(s)/seller(s) involved.

If using the estate agent's solicitor, the fees for drawing up the preliminary contract would normally be included in the estate agent's commission, but it's worth confirming this with the agent when you first meet with them. If you have engaged an independent solicitor to conduct both the preliminary and final contracts, then you would typically pay 50 per cent of the fee upon signing the preliminary contract and the remaining 50 per cent after concluding the final contract.

You should also remember to take away the signed preliminary contract. If you don't have a copy in English, I'd suggest that you ask your agent to get it translated for you, or alternatively find a local translator yourself to do the translation.

Fixing the date for the final contract (notary deed)

In the preliminary contract, it's normal practice to state the date (agreed between buyer and seller) for the final contract (also known as the **notary deed**) to be signed. This is also the date by which the final payment on the property must be made.

If your purchase requires the set-up of a company, it's a good idea to set this date at least 30 days, if not more, in the future to allow for the average time it takes to set up a company (20 days). Again, as I mentioned earlier, some organisations can set up a company much faster than this – in which case, you could set a date within 30 days.

It's a combination of personal preference (depending on your financial situation and how much time you need to get the money) and agreement with the seller. For example, if the seller is in a hurry it might be difficult to delay it by more than 30 days.

Additional terms in the preliminary contract

If you are purchasing a new-build or a recently renovated property – here's a tip for you. Ensure that you have thoroughly inspected the property and if you have found any issues, add these in a separate contract tied to the preliminary contract. For example, there may be some building work that the developer must complete before you can accept the property. Hence you need to ensure that this is clearly stated in the supplemental contract. Just make it clear to your agent that this is what you want, and they should do this for you and cover the cost within their commission (i.e. at no additional cost to you).

Signing the final contract (notary deed)

There are a couple of ways of dealing with the final contract. One is to give power of attorney to someone you trust to sign the paperwork on your behalf. The other is to come to Bulgaria yourself. Clearly, such an important stage in the purchase process would benefit from your presence, so do try to make every effort to sign the final contract yourself. If you are purchasing a new property it's even more important, especially if you did tie additional points to the preliminary contract. In such a case you will have to inspect the property and be sure that the issues have been addressed.

I would advise you to arrange for the final contract to be translated in English, as this will become the final binding legal contract – and the preliminary contract will no longer be valid. Do be sure to read through the whole contract. Check that it includes all the rooms, land etc. that you understand the property to have, and do check that the declared purchase price is stated correctly.

Purchase price: higher or lower?

Perhaps one of the most controversial subjects when buying property in Bulgaria, is the issue of which price is declared in the notary deed.

Every property in Bulgaria will have a government tax evaluation price assigned to it, which is always far removed from the actual market value of the property. What many sellers do in Bulgaria is ask for the amount declared in the notary deed to be close to this government tax evaluation price. Why, you may ask? To avoid paying larger taxes on the sale of the property is the principal reason – and you may also be buying from someone who themselves was coerced to declare the lower price when they bought the property!

Many real estate agent websites will suggest that this is standard practice in Bulgaria. In fact, it *is* standard practice. Everyone in Bulgaria is aware of this situation and little is being done to curb this.

Some lawyers will tell you this is simply illegal, whilst others will suggest that it relates to a loophole in the law. In 2008, it is still common practice for 90 per cent of developers of new property developments to ask you to declare the lower price on the notary deed. However, if you agree to pay the 20 per cent VAT on the new property, many developers will agree to declare the full market price you are paying for the property in the notary deed.

Be aware that if you declare the lower price, then when you come to sell the property, if sold for the real market price, you will be incurring a larger tax payment, since the tax payable will be based on the difference between the market sale price and the price you declared in the notary deed.

It is very important to seek both the assistance of a lawyer and an account-ant to advise you on the best practice for your particular situation.

Transferring the money for the final payment

Prior to your trip to Bulgaria, it is advisable to arrange for the final pay-ment (plus a little extra) to be transferred to your local currency account in Bulgaria. You can then withdraw this money conveniently when you arrive in Bulgaria.

Sometimes you will find that the seller insists on receiving the final pay-ment in cash – at other times, a telegraphic transfer either from your home bank account, or your local Bulgarian bank account, will be accept-able. The reason why a transfer from your home bank account (in your home country) may not be acceptable is that the receiver generally incurs a cost for receiving foreign currency – and quite naturally does not want to pay these fees.

However you decide to transfer the money, just ensure that you check any related bank charges for the transaction and that you have sufficient funds in your bank account to cover these charges. You may also wish to grant your lawyer in Bulgaria power of attorney over your accounts, so that they can act on your behalf.

If you are buying a property which requires a company, then it's better to get your lawyer to transfer the money from your personal bank account (in Bulgaria) to your company bank account, and then manage the transfer of the money from your company account to the sellers.

Can I sign the contract now?

So, you've transferred the money to your local Bulgarian bank account, you've got an English copy of the final contract and you've checked that your property is ready. Can you sign the contract? Yes? Well, let's say no. Let's say that your property still has some issues. What can you do? In such a situation, it is common to prepare what's called a 'protocol' or additional document that is tied to the final contract – which usually declares a fixed amount of time by which the issues will be resolved.

To cover such a scenario it is also quite common to reserve a certain amount of money to cover these issues being addressed. If the agreed date arrives, and the issues are not addressed then this money is not paid to the seller, and is, instead returned to the buyer as some form of compensation. Typically, when the final contract is first checked with yourself, the agent and the appointed solicitor, if you feel the need for an additional 'protocol' document, then you would request the solicitor draft this and then tie it to the final contract.

All parties, buyer and seller, must be present in front of the notary public to sign the final contract. This can be a quite large meeting, with what appears to be every man and his dog present. But don't despair, it's quite normal to have several parties present at such a meeting.

Such a meeting would typically include:

1. Buyer(s)

2. Seller(s)

3. Agent/local estate agent

4. Developer (for new build/off-plan development)

5. Solicitor

6. Notary public

7. Translator

At every stage, a translator will explain what each document is before you sign it.

After signing the final contract, you would then either:

◆ Proceed by giving the cash to the seller (which you withdrew earlier from the bank), or

◆ Proceed with the telegraphic transfer to the seller's bank account

At this point, you should also expect to get the key(s) for the property – or, at least arrange to pick up the keys the same day.

Congratulations! You are now the proud owner of your very own Bulgarian property. Now, you just need to pay some fees / taxes which are in the form of a municipal tax, a court tax and the notary public fee. These typically breakdown as follows:

Municipal tax (equivalent to the 'stamp duty' in the UK)	2%
Local court tax for registering the title deeds	0.1%
Notary public fee	0.1% – 1.5%

Percentages are expressed in terms of the property purchase price.

After paying the notary's fees you can expect to receive a receipt before you leave the notary public's office. If you have not used the estate agent's own solicitor, you will also have the legal costs to pay associated with the preparation of the preliminary contract and the notary deed, and the checks made on the property. This will vary according to the solicitor used. You can typically expect to pay 1% of the purchase price for a good solicitor, to cover all the legal costs of buying the property. The minimum charge would be typically 300–500 euros.

BULSTAT registration

If you are foreigner buying property in Bulgaria and have not registered a Bulgarian company, you are required to make a separate BULSTAT registration within 7 days of purchasing a property. This requirement was effective from the 11th August 2005 when the BULSTAT Register Act came into effect. This process would typically be managed by your solicitor, but you should check that this has been arranged to avoid any associated penalty for late registration.

Permission to use the property

If you are purchasing a **new** house/apartment, then before you can move in you need to ensure that a certificate that provides you with 'permission to use' the property has been issued. It is illegal to live in the property until this certificate has been granted.

The normal sequence is that an 'Act 15' will be issued first, once the building itself has been constructed. This 'Act 15' usually requires the signatures of the owner(s). The developer would contact the owner(s) to let them know when this 'Act 15' is ready to sign.

The owners are expected to sign this 'Act 15' to show their acceptance of the building and construction work. It is at this time that the owners have the right to express any concerns over the building or construction work. The 'Act 15' will also describe any work not done or not finished to a quality standard, and any repairs pending.

A subsequent stage requires various authorities, including those responsible for electricity, water, fire, construction control etc. to approve the building construction and to agree that it falls under the various regulations and technical requirements. The document issued at this stage is referred to as 'Act 16' and must also be signed by the owner(s).

Following the issue of 'Act 16', the final document to be issued is the 'permission to use' certificate as previously mentioned. This document would generally be signed by the chief architect of the municipality – and would also include the names of the owners.

Ideally, you should insist on the developer providing this 'permission to use' certificate prior to you signing the notary deed. However, this may not always be possible due to building or other bureaucratic delays.

Prior to signing the notary deed your solicitor may advise you to add a clause in a separate (but related) 'protocol' document that states the date by which this certificate must be obtained by the developer. If the certificate is not obtained by that date, you can negotiate a certain percentage of the final payment being held back and have this amount stated in the contract. This means that the seller / developer must refund this agreed amount back to you if they have not met their obligations within the stipulated period.

What you may find is that an amount – somewhere between three to ten per cent – is held by the notary public, who has instructions to pass this money to the seller / developer once the certificate of fitness for living has been issued – provided it is by the agreed date. It would then fall on the notary public to send this money back to you, should this not be the case. It may be that your solicitor insists that the notary deed is not signed (and money paid) until the developer has received the 'permission to use' certificate and that this is stated clearly in the contract – to ensure that you are taking possession of a habitable property.

5

Paying for your property

Whilst I have already covered the basics when purchasing your property, I'd like to cover a few practical issues in more detail – and also talk about how to finance your property purchase in Bulgaria.

At present, there are only a few organisations within the UK that will provide mortgages for the purchase of property in Bulgaria. This will change in time, just as it has for other areas such as France and Spain. As an emerging market, Bulgaria has yet to convince the majority of financial establishments that it's a worthy location.

So, you've found your dream home but don't have the money to pay for it. What can you do? First of all, don't give up!

HOW TO FINANCE YOUR PURCHASE

There are a number of approaches that you can take to finance your purchase. By far one of the most popular approaches is to re-mortgage your own home to release the equity. This can sometimes provide a considerable amount of money for investment purposes.

Simply contact your mortgage provider and ask them about their additional borrowing facilities (against your mortgage). They will be more than happy to assist you – after all, they will be increasing their own income and stand to gain from your interest payments!

However, if you are not this fortunate or have already spent the money you have released from the equity in your home, you will have to consider other options. Perhaps you can borrow some money from friends or family? You could also consider releasing any money that you may have tied up in shares, savings accounts, ISA's etc.

The other option, although less favourable, is to consider applying for a personal loan. Personal loans are offered by a large number of organisations who compete heavily on the interest rates – with the UK offering rates as low as 6.6 per cent in 2008.

When considering such additional financial obligations, you do of course need to ensure you can afford the payments (foremost) and that you can reasonably predict a return on your investment that is substantially above the interest rate of your loan. In Bulgaria, more and more banks are providing mortgages for foreigners. It is well worth investigating these options as the packages do vary and are becoming more competitive. In 2008, interest rates vary between approximately 7 and 10 per cent.

Finally, there are overseas mortgage specialists who can organise mortgages in many countries. For example, Conti Financial Services (www. mortgagesoverseas.com) now provide finance options to purchase property in Bulgaria provided, as do MoneySprite (www.moneysprite.com) and BulgarianHomeLoans (www.BulgarianHomeLoans.com)

SUMMARY OF FINANCING OPTIONS

In summary, then, you can look at the following sources for generating the money to purchase your property in Bulgaria:

◆ Your personal savings, ISA funds, premium bonds, fixed deposit certificates etc.

◆ Your stock market shares

◆ A low interest (or no interest) loan from friends or family members

◆ Additional borrowing on your mortgage (sometimes referred to as 'flexible loans')

◆ A personal loan

◆ If in a two-car family, the sale of one of the cars (a small price to pay, perhaps!)

◆ Approaching a bank in Bulgaria for a mortgage (e.g. Alpha Bank, Piraues Bank, First Investment Bank, United Bulgarian Bank and the Bulgarian American Credit Bank)

◆ Approaching a bank in your own country for a mortgage on a property in Bulgaria

◆ In extreme cases, when you want to 'live the dream', the cash remaining from the sale of your own house!

◆ Contacting an overseas mortgage specialist (e.g. Conti Financial Services, Moneysprite and BulgarianHomeLoans)

PROFILING THE PAYMENTS

When it comes to purchasing your Bulgarian property, remember that you are generally not paying for it all at once – but generally follow a pattern of an initial 10 per cent deposit and 90 per cent on completion after 30-60 days. What this means is that you can effectively profile your payments, and plan ahead, by only releasing the money when you need it. It also means that you can play the currency markets a little. Let me explain.

PLAYING THE CURRENCY MARKETS

When properties are advertised in Bulgaria, they are generally advertised in either US dollars or euros. What this means is that the prices as far as UK pounds are concerned, are fluctuating constantly.

If buying in euros, keeping a close eye on the exchange rate – on a daily basis – can actually save you money. It could, in theory, cost you more money – but that's why you need to look at the situation with some degree of intelligence.

Let's say that just before you sign the preliminary contract the exchange rate between the pound and the euro is 1.47 (i.e. to buy euros, £1 sterling buys you 1.47 euros). Let's also assume for arguments sake, that you are purchasing a property at 100,000 euros. This means that at the time of signing the preliminary contract the property costs you £68,027.

Now, you only have to pay 10 per cent (approximately) at this time, which will cost you £6,803.

Let's assume that you have agreed to settle the final payment within 60 days. That effectively gives you 60 days to watch the currency market – with a view to buying a rate, at some point in those 60 days, which is greater than or equal to the rate when you signed the preliminary contract – i.e. >= 1.47.

When you purchased the euros at the time of signing the preliminary contract, it is worth determining whether the euro is on an upward trend. You can check this quite easily by viewing the intra-day and month euro rates on the BBC website (www.bbc.co.uk). By monitoring the mid-rate published on this website, you can estimate whether the euro is currently on an upward or downward trend. If on an upward trend, you can buy a forward rate with a currency exchange company or take the slightly riskier approach of buying a spot rate when you feel that it has reached the peak.

It's a guessing game, for sure, but one that could ultimately save you money, and lower the purchase price of the property you are buying. If, for arguments sake, the rate rises to 1.5 by the time you are close to signing the final contract you could buy this rate and pay the remainder 90,000 euros at a cost of £60,000.

If you had bought those 90,000 euros at 1.47, that would have cost you £61,224. So, you have saved yourself £1,224 – just by 'playing the market'.

Be warned though, it can work either way. If you want to play it safe and avoid a situation where you might lose on the exchange rate later on, buy all the euros at the same time when you are paying the 10 per cent deposit on your property.

6

Renovating your property

Depending on the type of property you have purchased you may require further renovation work. You therefore need to consider whether to do it yourself or to find a local builder.

QUOTES

When getting any building work done, it's important to get at least two quotes and if possible three – so that you are in a better position to understand the local prices and can feel more confident that you are being quoted a fair price for the work.

A typical new-build may be without floors (as mentioned earlier in the book), bathroom, kitchen, etc. so it's important that you find the best possible price for all these 'extras'. Also, consider requesting the quotation be translated into your own language (e.g. English) so that you are clear on every point. Remember, the more detailed the quote (and what you ask to be quoted) the more accurate (in theory) the quote will be.

FINDING A BUILDER

It may seem daunting at first, due to language problems, and lack of information, but you should be perfectly capable of finding a local builder from a number of sources. Perhaps the best source is someone that you know that has recommended a particular builder. Other sources include:

- Asking the agency that you have bought the property from

- If using a UK-based agent, ask them if they provide building/renovation services

- Ask a neighbour, you will generally find Bulgarians are very friendly and willing to help (you may need a translator)

- The growing number of internet-based forums, set up by people who are either living or investing in Bulgaria (Appendix H)

WHAT CAN YOU EXPECT TO PAY?

Outlined below are some example costs (based on actual quotes in 2004) to provide you with an indicative set of costs, to allow you to budget your own renovation work.

Service	Price
Installation of tiles (e.g. bathroom)	13 Leva /m^2
Installation of boiler	29 Leva
Fixing boiler board/switch	13 Leva
Installation of shower cabin	40–100 Leva
Delivery and installation of ventilator	75 Leva
Installation of suspended ceiling	26 Leva/m^2
Installation of bathroom accessories	10 Leva per item
Delivery and installation of shaver point	50 Leva
Fixing walls with latex	9.60 Leva/m^2
Installation and testing shower mixer	19.50 Leva
Installation of laminate floor	5 Leva/m^2
Installation of skirting board	5 Leva/m^2
Installation of wash basin	35 Leva
Installation of door bell	18 Leva
Loading, transportation, disposal costs	380 Leva

[Note: These costs are based on actual prices quoted in 2007, and are provided as an illustration to guide you through the estimation work on your renovation project.]

7

Tax considerations

If you are going to buy a property in Bulgaria then it is well worth spending some time understanding the basics of the tax system. You will need to consider various taxes depending on whether you are buying, selling or renting your property out. This chapter presents the basic facts about tax, so that you can at least establish what they are – and when you meet with a Bulgarian accountant (which I strongly recommend) you have at least a basis from which to start your discussions.

You will find so many contradictions about the tax system in Bulgaria, just as I did whilst researching the subject – as no two sources of information ever appear to be the same! The subject of capital gains tax is perhaps one of the most contentious subjects on the internet forums on Bulgaria – with such a variety of opinions. However, my research has shown that Bulgaria does not have a capital gains tax, in the same way that we do in the UK. So, read on and prepare to be enlightened!

PROPERTY PURCHASE TAX

Property purchase taxes include those taxes payable on the purchase of your property:

1. the municipal tax (equivalent to the stamp duty) at 2 per cent of the purchase price and

2. the local court tax of 0.1 per cent of the purchase price.

These taxes are paid after you have signed the notary deed and are usually paid in Leva.

ANNUAL TAX

There is also an annual tax to pay on your property, with an additional 'garbage' tax for the collection of rubbish from your home. The annual property tax for individuals is 0.15% of the tax evaluation price for a property (or regulated land). There is no property tax to pay for unregulated land.

If the property / land is owned by a Bulgarian company, then the 0.15% tax is payable on the price declared for the asset in the company's balance sheet.

Garbage tax varies according to the local municipality in which the property is situated. Typically, allow between 0.15% - 0.7% for this tax.

TAX TO PAY ON RENTAL PROPERTIES

If you are renting out your property to tenants then you must also take into account the tax payable on the profit that you make from this rental. As a resident of Bulgaria, you will be taxed according to the income tax table. If you are a non-resident, then you will be taxed at a flat rate of 15 per cent on the taxable profit (i.e. a withholding tax). You must also consider any additional tax payable in your country of residence based on your worldwide income.

PERSONAL TAX

The tax that you pay will depend on your residency status. As a resident, income tax is now based on a flat tax rate of 10% from January 2008. Prior to this, income tax was based on a progressive scale of tax rates from 0 to 24%.

In recent years, the Bulgarian government has consistently made changes to income tax rates annually. Therefore, you must always check the current tax legislation or contact a Bulgarian accountant to get the latest information.

If you are a non-resident then you are liable to pay a 10 per cent withholding tax on any rental income you receive on your Bulgarian property.

If you are a resident of the United Kingdom, for example, you must also consider the fact that there may be additional tax to pay to the UK government. After paying any income tax on the rental income to the Bulgarian government you may have to consider paying any remaining income tax to the UK government, depending on which tax bracket you fall into. This is because, as a UK-resident, you are liable to pay tax on your worldwide income. My advice would be to get a good accountant!

A double taxation agreement exists between the UK and Bulgaria – hence the split of taxes described above. If you are not from the UK, you will need to check whether there is a double taxation agreement between your country and Bulgaria. At the time of writing, double taxation agreements have been established for the following countries:

Albania, Armenia, Austria, Belarus, Belgium, China, Croatia, Cyprus, Czech Republic, Denmark, Finland, France, Georgia, Germany, Greece, Hungary, India, Indonesia, Republic of Ireland, Israel, Italy, Japan, Kazakhstan, Lebanon, Luxembourg, Macedonia, Malta, Morocco, Moldova, The Netherlands, Norway, North Korea, Poland, Portugal, Romania, Russian Federation, Spain, Singapore, Slovak Republic, South Korea, Sweden, Switzerland, Syria, Thailand, Turkey, Ukraine, United Kingdom, Vietnam, Yugoslavia, Zimbabwe.

In order to reduce your tax payments you should of course seek independent tax advice from a qualified accountant, preferably with some international experience.

If you are buying as a couple, putting the property in both your names can help by splitting the tax liability. Since you would benefit from the fact that each of you has a personal tax allowance – and it may be that one of you is also a lower rate tax payer. With the property in both your names, the income you receive can be divided equally between you, and then you are each taxed separately on your equal share of the income.

◆ TOP TIP ◆

Find an accountant in Bulgaria before you buy a property and check what the tax implications are on buying, renting and selling the property (as applicable). These tax regulations are likely to change, so you also need to keep informed of any changes.

Also, in your own country, check with an accountant on the tax implications within your country.

I should point out here, of course, that these personal tax liabilities may not be relevant if you have bought a property under a company. This is because the purchase of the property was under a corporate structure and not an individual one. Hence you would need to consider the corporate tax liability instead (see page 67).

Taxes on the sale of property

As a non-resident of Bulgaria

Bulgarian source income of non-residents derived from dividends, interest, capital gains, lease payments, technical service fees and royalties are subject to a withholding tax of between 7 and 10 per cent. The tax rate may be reduced by an applicable double taxation treaty. Dividends distributed by resident companies to resident individuals and non-commercial entities are subject to 7 per cent withholding tax.

Bulgaria, strictly speaking, does not have a capital gains tax as we do in the UK. However, if you are a non-resident of Bulgaria and you sell your Bulgarian property, then you do have to pay this withholding tax. This tax is paid on the difference between the purchase price and the selling price of the property.

However, this does not change the position with respect to the capital gains tax on your worldwide income in your country of residence. For example, as a UK-resident you would still be liable to the capital gains you make on the sale of your property in Bulgaria. If you are a higher rate tax payer, then this would be taxable at the rate of 40 per cent. This, of course, could be offset against what you have already paid in Bulgaria provided it is within the terms of the double taxation agreement.

You need to remember that this tax only applies if you purchased a property as a foreign individual and not if you have purchased under a corporate structure. Therefore it generally applies to the majority of apartments (that exclude land). Non-residents are liable only for their income derived from Bulgarian sources.

As a resident of Bulgaria

Bulgarian tax residents are taxed on their worldwide income. Irrespective of their citizenship, individuals are considered Bulgarian tax residents if they have permanent residence in the country (i.e. personal links such as family or a permanent home) or reside in the country for more than 183 days in any 365-day period, in which case the individual becomes a Bulgarian tax resident for the calendar year in which the 183-day period has exceeded.

A resident is not liable to pay any tax on the capital gains from the sale of one property within a financial year. The property must be for the resident's sole residential use and is not being rented out to tenants.

If a tax resident in Bulgaria has owned property for at least five years then the resident is also entitled to sell up to two real estate entities (e.g. land, office, residential dwelling) in a financial year, without incurring any tax liabilities. Otherwise you are taxed according to the income tax regulations, based on the difference between the purchase price and the selling price.

General advice

As laws are changing you are advised to check the situation with a solicitor in Bulgaria prior to the sale of your property. I would go as far as suggesting you check these facts even before buying your property so that you have some idea of any future tax liabilities you may incur.

As no one can predict the future, it is difficult to know how the next few years will affect the taxation in Bulgaria. The only form of guidance that you can take is to look to the other Eastern European countries that have recently entered the EU (e.g. Latvia, Estonia, Lithuania etc.) and see what changes they incur. This can then be used at least as some indication of what may follow in other Eastern European countries.

CORPORATE TAX

Corporate taxation is governed by the Corporate Income Tax Act. In general, business profits are subject to corporate income tax. If you have purchased a property (or land) under a Bulgarian company, then you will have to consider the tax implications on the **sale** of your property.

The corporate tax on **profit** is currently set at 10 per cent. This means when it comes to selling a property (or land), the government will take 10 per cent of the company taxable profit at the end of the financial year. The financial year in Bulgaria is equivalent to the calendar year – 1 January to 31 December. Similarly, the tax on your rental income will currently be based on the corporate tax rate of 10 per cent. The tax you pay will be on the company taxable profit on that rental income.

Almost every year changes are made in the legislation by the Parliament and the tax rate is also changed. From January 2007 the Bulgarian government reduced the corporation tax from 15 to 10 per cent. There may be further reductions beyond that in the future.

VAT

I know what you are thinking – they surely don't have VAT in Bulgaria too, do they? I'm afraid so.

If you have purchased your property as an individual (i.e. not under a corporate structure) then VAT will not be chargeable to the buyer when you sell your property **unless** you have had to register for VAT as an individual (e.g. if you are selling properties as an individual). However, if you have purchased a property as a company, then when you come to sell your property (if that's your intention) you may have to add VAT to your sale price. It depends on whether you have registered your company for VAT purposes. Currently, you must register your company for VAT if the turnover (over the last 12 months) exceeds 50,000 Leva (approximately 25,500 euros).

It is therefore unlikely that you would charge VAT on the sale of your first property. However, for the second (and subsequent property sales) after you have registered your company for VAT purposes, you would need to add VAT and charge this to the buyer. You would also add VAT to any rental charges if the property rental is not invoiced for an individual's residential use (e.g. if it was used as office space). VAT is currently set at 20 per cent. So it's actually higher than it is in the UK (17.5 per cent).

From January 2007 VAT is payable on the purchase of regulated land if the seller is registered for VAT purposes (where the seller could be a company or an individual).

But won't VAT put the potential buyer off buying my property?

The fact that you will have to charge VAT on the sale of your property (if you have registered for VAT) obviously raises the concern of how it might affect the price of your property in the market place. As it clearly has the potential to make it appear to be up to 20 per cent higher than properties of a similar type.

This is one of the drawbacks of setting up a company structure when you buy a property in Bulgaria, particularly if you are planning to sell it one day. However, there are ways of addressing this.

The most common way is to ensure that the buyer is buying under a corporate structure **and** is VAT registered. That way your *output* tax can be offset against the buyers *input* tax. At present, if you had to buy the property under a Bulgarian company and you are selling to another foreign individual, it is likely that the buyer will have to form a company anyway.

You do need to take into account that this practice of having to buy property under a company (for foreign individuals) is likely to change in the future. It is only a question of time before foreign ownership of land is likely to become accessible. An obvious advantage to Bulgaria, of relaxing the foreign ownership, is that it is likely to result in increased foreign investment in the country – which will ultimately help to drive the economy further forward.

8
Property and contents insurance

If you have bought a property to rent out, then you do need to give careful consideration to contents insurance. There are a number of both local and international insurance companies in Bulgaria. The process of applying for insurance can seem more complex when compared to how it is dealt with in the UK. However, this is primarily because you will need to provide a more detailed account of the risk that you want to cover.

BASIC COVER

The cover is measured in terms of risk. For the typical basic cover you would be looking at areas including:

◆ Fire

◆ Lightning

◆ Explosion

◆ Implosion

◆ Falling objects (such as aerials for example)

EXTENDED COVER

To provide further protection (i.e. for increased risk) then you may typically expect to cover risks including:

◆ Storm

◆ Torrential rain

◆ Flood

◆ Landslide

◆ Earthquake

◆ Fire caused by earthquake

◆ Tidal waves

ADDITIONAL COVER

You will also find companies that offer additional cover for risks including:

◆ Theft

◆ Vandalism

◆ Breakages of glass / windows

WHAT KIND OF INFORMATION DO I NEED TO PROVIDE?

When completing an application form for property insurance, you would be typically asked for information such as:

Building insurance
◆ Name and address

◆ Insured property details (how many floors it is on, which floor you occupy)

◆ Type of building

◆ Whether it's private or rented

◆ The occupation of the building (whether it's permanent, seasonal etc.)

◆ The type of construction (e.g. material used for inner/outer walls)

◆ The type of roof construction (steel, wooden, tiled etc.)

◆ The number and type of material used for the doors and windows

◆ Details of any fire alarms installed

◆ Details of any security system installed and security company used (even to the extent of providing the response time from that security company!)

Contents insurance

◆ Household furnishings

◆ Jewellery and precious metals in the building

◆ Art work

◆ Antiques (e.g. with historical value)

◆ Technical devices and appliances

◆ Other items (to be specifically insured)

Other areas on the application

You will also be expected to declare whether there has been any loss within the last five years or so. In some cases you may have to provide a survey of the building. This is particularly important if you have purchased a potential unstable property (of considerable age).

WHAT CAN I EXPECT TO PAY FOR CONTENTS INSURANCE?

This can vary significantly due to the difference in buildings, contents and risks to be covered. You can typically expect to pay between 400–450 Leva annually (excluding theft cover) for an average two/three bedroom apartment – but you should obviously shop around for the best deal.

HOW CAN I GO ABOUT TAKING OUT INSURANCE AND FINDING A COMPANY?

If you are renting out your property then my advice is to use a property management company to assist you with the insurance. They will generally know the best insurance companies to use and will already have experience in this area. You would need to sign a contract with the property management company that gives them the ability to sign contracts (such as insurance contracts) on your behalf. This takes the burden away from you and puts it into the hands of the professionals.

If this route is not appropriate then you can consider approaching one of the insurance companies on a high street in one of the major cities, for example, in Sofia or Varna. I have provided the names of some insurance companies in Appendix I to assist you. Alternatively, you can approach some of the internet forums where a growing community of foreign nationals share their experiences – and you will find people who are already living in Bulgaria who have taken out insurance and can share the details of their experience, contacts etc. with you. This kind of 'community' is invaluable when you are very much in the dark as to how things work in a foreign country.

9
Furnishing your property

Having successfully purchased your home and assuming that you haven't purchased one that's already furnished – you're probably going to need some help in furnishing it. For those of you who have bought a home declared to be to 'Bulgarian standards' you may also require the assistance of some local builders to install your floors, bathroom and kitchen.

So where to start? As I've indicated in several places in this book, there is a growing community, particularly in England, of people who help each other through internet-based forums. Perhaps one of the most popular being the www.mybulgaria.info website, in which members really do share their experiences, good and bad, to help each other. You will find numerous postings in this forum of people who have used local companies to furnish their homes, and can contact these people through the forum for contact details.

A couple of good stores that between them cover the majority of electrical equipment you'll require and furnishings in general are Technomarket and Metro. These can be found in the major cities, and provide an excellent choice. In general, you should expect to pay 1 Leva / km for delivery costs, and in most cities delivery can be expected either the next day or certainly within a couple of days or so if the items are in stock. However, you may find that you are paying on average between 10-20 Leva for the delivery.

It's also possible to approach the local companies to furnish your apartment or house for you. Here, you provide the company with the details of your property – if possible take them round the property yourself – and get them to produce a quote. It's best to request a medium price for the floors, tiles, equipment etc. as there can be a tendency to assume you are willing to pay for the imported goods, which are generally more expensive. If you are working to a tight budget and perhaps plan to rent the properties, you may wish to consider locally-made furniture. This is of a generally good standard and can also be made to order.

I've heard it said that you can furnish an average two-bedroom apartment in Bulgaria for approximately 3,000 euros. Of course, prices and quality vary – but you should find it possible to finish and furnish your property for considerably less cost than the equivalent in England.

If you have bought an average two-bedroom apartment (e.g. 100 metre square) that requires all the finishing work – e.g. requires floor, bathroom, kitchen, furnishing, air-conditioning etc. – then you should really set aside a budget upwards of 12,000 euros, to furnish your apartment to a reasonable standard.

GAS OR ELECTRIC OVEN?

In Bulgaria, electricity tends to be the more common option for ovens/hobs, as gas is not generally available in properties in the same way that it is in the UK, for example.

If you want to use gas, you would have to purchase gas cylinders – which may not be a convenient option if you are planning to rent your property out. However, gas would be considered a more economical option.

WHAT CAN I EXPECT TO PAY?

Outlined below is a list of prices for various items that you may require for your Bulgarian property – with average prices. Clearly, prices vary according to quality and choice.

Item	Price (Leva)	Price equivalent (€ Euro)
Aircon unit	450 – 2000	230 – 1023
Toilet	200 – 400	102 – 205
Shower cubicle	800 – 2000	409 – 1023
Shower head/control	100 – 500	51 – 256
Fire detector	100 – 150	51 – 77
Fitted kitchen	1200 – 2000	614 – 1023
Kitchen boiler	400 – 500	205 – 256
Bathroom boiler	300 – 400	153 – 205
Fridge	500 – 900	256 – 460
Washing machine	450 – 800	230 – 409
Coffee table	200 – 300	102 – 153
Double bed + mattress	900 – 1200	460 – 614
Wardrobe	500 – 1200	256 – 614
Bedside cabinet	60 – 120	31 – 61
Television (26")	300 – 400	153 – 205
Dining table + 6 chairs	1000 – 1500	511 – 767
Oven	400 – 700	205 – 358
Oven hob	400 – 650	205 – 332
Extractor fan	300 – 600	153 – 307
Kitchen sink	150 – 500	77 – 256
Clothes hanger	150 – 300	77 – 153
Sofa bed	800 – 2000	409 – 1023

Prices assume an exchange rate of 1.955 Leva to €1 EUR.

BOILERS

In Bulgaria, it's common to see the boilers exposed when you enter a bathroom. This can look a little unsightly to the average Western eye, but is considered quite normal in Bulgaria. You can of course pay more to have the boiler concealed or another option is to consider having the boiler placed above the bathroom door, if there is sufficient space.

Gas central heating is uncommon in Bulgaria, and the water in the majority of homes is heated through the electric boiler system. Water in the kitchen is also generally heated by a boiler, which can be concealed underneath the kitchen sink. Do consult with specialists to ensure that you are choosing the most economical form of boiler. Whilst it's easy to be tempted by the low prices of some of the locally-made boilers, you do need to understand the cost of running these boilers.

If you are renting your property out on short-term rentals this becomes even more important as you are probably including the price of heating in your rental, and must therefore reduce your exposure to large heating bills as best you can.

A WASHING MACHINE IN THE BATHROOM?

One noticeable observation that you will make if you are buying a home that is already furnished, is the strong likelihood of a washing machine in the bathroom.

To the majority of us in the West, this feels a little odd – and certainly not the most obvious place for your washing machine. In Eastern Europe, including Bulgaria, it is seen to be more common to find the washing machine in the bathroom. Kitchens in Eastern Europe are generally smaller than the ones in the West, so its more about finding somewhere where there is space for it. Naturally, if you are buying a new house/apartment, and there is room, there's no reason why you can't arrange to have the washing machine plumbed into the kitchen.

AIR CONDITIONING AND HEATING

If you have bought a property on the Black Sea Coast, it's advisable to install air conditioning. It does get rather hot in the summer months, and would be money well spent. As with the boilers, seek professional advice on what type of air conditioning unit would be the most economical for your needs.

Some air conditioning units also provide the ability to heat your rooms. So if you are looking for a combined heating and cooling solution, expect to pay more for the air conditioning units. It will save you space, as the alternatives would include under-floor heating or radiators. Central heating is not common in Bulgaria, and new properties tend to lack any heating – so do expect to find a solution yourself or pay the developer more to find a solution for you. Good brands include Panasonic, Samsung, Toshiba and LG. Do be wary of those brands that are considerably cheaper. Also remember that you get what you pay for! You would typically expect to install a larger aircon unit in the main living area (perhaps a 5.8kW unit) and smaller aircon units in the bedrooms (for example, around 3.0kW).

If you are looking for a more economical solution, with lower power consumption, you may want to consider an air conditioning unit with an 'inverter' which draws less current from the electrical supply. Toshiba's air conditioners come with this feature as standard. Do expect to pay more for air conditioners with an 'inverter', but consider the savings to be gained from less power consumption.

If you are looking for a cheaper solution for heating (at least cheaper purchase costs) then consider either the fan heaters or the oil-based radiators. These can cost anything upwards of about 30 Leva for the fan heaters, and from 80 Leva upwards for the oil-based electric radiators. Central heating is not so common currently – and is more available in Sofia and just starting to come into Varna.

So when buying a home, do not naturally assume that it will have central heating, as you would tend to assume in Western Europe or America, for example.

10

Paying the bills for your property

You can typically expect to pay the standard utility bills, which include:

◆ Electricity

◆ Water

◆ Telephone

Whether you are living in your property or renting it out, you may wish to consider setting up a direct debit payment with your local bank – so that the key utility bills are paid automatically every month. Most banks should at least provide this service for the payment of electricity and water bills.

Properties also have an annual tax levied on them which you also need to make arrangements to pay (as previously mentioned in the tax section of this book – see Chapter 7). You could, alternatively, arrange for a rental/property management company to mange the bill payments as part of their service to you if you are renting your property out. But the more you can organise yourself, the less you will need to pay the property management company – at least in theory!

Telephone calls, compared to Western Europe and America, can be more expensive as the telecom industry is far less competitive. Therefore the cost of your telephone calls can easily work out more expensive unless you take steps to keep it under control.

ELECTRICITY PRICES

From January 2007, the price of electrical power in Bulgaria was divided into two components:

- price of electric distribution/transfer/and
- price for electric power sale/supply

In line with the legislative requirements, these are indicated on electricity invoices separately.

Electricity prices (sale/supply) to household customers (excluding VAT) from 1st July 2007, from EON Bulgaria:

Time of day	Cost (per kilowatt hour) for sale/supply
Daytime	0.07657 Leva
Night-time	0.02927 Leva

Electricity prices (transfer/distribution) to all users (excluding VAT) from EON Bulgaria:

Type of voltage	Cost (per kilowatt hour) for distribution
Low voltage	0.01634 Leva
Middle voltage	0.05458 Leva

You should of course check with the electricity company for the latest prices as these are subject to change.

An average household can expect an electricity bill of somewhere between 60-70 Leva a month and a bill of between 150-200 Leva during the winter months. Clearly this depends on a number of factors, but this gives you an approximate idea of the typical costs.

WATER PRICES

Water rates are quite reasonable but in some areas of Bulgaria you cannot expect to have running water 24 hours a day! In the more developed cities, such as Sofia and Varna, for example, this is less of an issue, but it is worth checking this before you buy your property!

As a guide to the water prices in Bulgaria, the water rates for households in Varna are 1.76 Leva per m^3. This rate varies according to region. An average household can expect a water bill of somewhere between 20-30 Leva a month.

11

Transferring money to Bulgaria

It is sensible to set up a local bank account in Bulgaria – preferably a euro account – since the majority of properties are advertised and sold in euros.

As you will probably be transferring money, not only for the property you are buying, but also for other costs, including builders' fees, materials, bill payments etc, it is well worth researching companies that can provide a convenient service for transferring money to and from Bulgaria. Your average high street bank does not offer you the best rate of exchange on currency, no matter what they tell you. You may pop into your local bank and be quoted a rate of 1.43 euros to the pound (for example), but find a specialist currency exchange company that can give you a rate of 1.48. That could be a significant saving for you, so it is well worth the time and effort exploring.

So what are the practical considerations when it comes to sending money to Bulgaria? The first point is to remember that it takes time to send money overseas. How long typically depends on the country and means by which you transfer. On average, you can expect the transaction to take anything from three days to seven days, from start to finish. The second point to consider is the transfer fee. Different organisations have different fee structures and it is well worth researching which one works for you.

TRANSFERRING YOUR MONEY USING AN INTERNET-BASED SERVICE

Let's take a look at XETrade, a service of Canada-based internet company XE.com that provides currency exchange services. The benefit with this service is that you can find excellent exchange rates and conduct the transaction completely on the internet without speaking to anyone.

This can be very convenient, especially if you are used to conducting your financial affairs on the internet and don't have the hang-ups that some people still have about performing financial transactions on the web. That said, it is worth researching the company that you are planning to use, especially for financial transactions. XE.com, for example, have been in business since 1993 and have been providing XETrade for over three years. So, how does XETrade work?

Setting up an account with XETrade

The first thing you need to do is to set up an account with XETrade.

1. Access their website **www.xe.com/fx/**

2. Choose the option to sign up for an account

3. Specify your first name, last name and email address

4. Read the agreement terms and conditions and select 'I agree' (assuming that you do agree with these terms and conditions)

5. Provide the login details for your desired account

6. Specify your contact details

7. Submit your application

You would be expected to fax a copy of this application to XETrade and also to supply fax copies of additional documents as requested. This can also be done electronically via a secure file transfer system. Full details of how to do this are given to you at the end of the 'sign up' process.

Setting up your Bulgarian bank account

Once you have successfully set up an XETrade account you will need to log in to the system and define the account that you want to transfer the money to in Bulgaria in Euros (EUR).

1. Select the option 'Wire Beneficiaries' under 'Account Maintenance' on the main menu

2. Click the button **Add New Wire Beneficiary**

3. Provide the name of the beneficiary (which would be your name, for example, but it must match the name that appears on the account)

4. Specify the name of your Bulgarian bank

5. Provide the bank account number and routing codes

6. Specify the bank's address details (address, city, country, province/state, postal code)

7. If there is an intermediate bank involved in the transfer, specify the details of this intermediary bank

8. Press the **Submit** button to complete the transaction

You may also find it useful to define additional beneficiaries if you are dealing with other organisations in Bulgaria. For example, if you are renting properties out, you could define the property management company as a beneficiary for any payments you need to wire to them. You will need to ensure that they can receive payments in Euros.

Transferring money to your Bulgarian bank account

If you follow these steps your money will be transferred to your Bulgarian bank account, generally within seven working days, from start to finish:

	Step	Tip
1	Log in to XETrade and choose the option **Basic Trade**.	**Basic trade** allows you to buy currency immediately.
2	Enter the amount that you are either wanting to sell, or wanting to buy.	I recommend choosing the option to **buy**.
3	Select the buying currency and selling currency.	If you are in the UK, you would typically expect to sell in pounds (GBP) sterling and buy euros (EUR).
4	Select the method by which you want to transfer the money (a) from XETrade to your beneficiary account and (b) from your bank to XETrade (to pay XETrade)	I would recommend **wire** for both.
5	Select the recipient (i.e. your Bulgarian bank account) from the drop down list and enter a reference code if you wish to.	This can be anything such as an invoice number, a note for your reference or nothing at all.
6	You will be presented with a page that shows the currency exchange rate.	Check this exchange rate and ensure that you are happy with this rate. You will also see the total cost of the transaction.
7	You then have 60 seconds to make a decision to buy the currency.	You can press the **Refresh Rates** button to retrieve the latest 'spot' rate. You can also choose to cancel the transaction at this point if you wish. This allows you to evaluate the rates risk free.
8	Confirm the trade by pressing the **Confirm Trade** button.	Once you are happy with the exchange rate, choose the option to confirm. The rate is locked in at this point and the trade is legally binding.
9	Wait for the confirmation email from XETrade that confirms the trade.	This would typically be emailed within 24 hours.
10	Log on to your personal bank account (via the internet) to transfer the funds to XETrade.	XETrade provide you with the bank account details of where to send the funds. The account details depend on whether you pay by BACS (internet transfers) or CHAPS.
11	Send the money from your personal bank account via BACS or CHAPS within the UK.	BACS takes between 3-5 days to clear with XETrade and CHAPS clears usually within 1 day.
12	Wait for a final email from XETrade which confirms that the funds have been transferred to the destination.	Once XETrade receive the payment from you they will then send the funds to your designated Bulgarian Euro bank account.

The final email you receive would look something like this:

Status	COMPLETED
Trade Type	Basic Trade
Deal Number	W11143587A
Customer Name	Jonathan White – Jonathan White
Customer Number	WEB123456
Value Date	April 12, 2004 at 11:47:36 AM PST (GMT-8)
You Bought	757.34 EUR
You Sold	507.92 GBP

So what does it cost?

There are three potential costs to consider:

1. The cost of sending a payment from your bank to XETrade (which is charged by your bank)

2. The cost of XETrade sending the funds to your Bulgarian bank account

3. The cost of your bank in Bulgaria receiving the funds

If you use internet banking and pay via BACS (in the UK) there is usually no charge. The cost of sending the money via XETrade to your Bulgarian bank account is usually less than £10, but it is not fixed. The XETrade wire fee is always quoted up front before you confirm your transaction.

The cost of receiving the money in your Bulgarian bank account can vary, but is quite typically 1 euro for every 1,000 euros transferred. Of course, you can also shop around for a bank in Bulgaria that does not charge for the receipt of foreign funds at all.

So, if you conduct all of these transactions on the internet, and you send 5,000 euros, you can typically expect a cost of:

1. 12 euros (XETrade charge – note this is just an illustration of a typical transaction)

2. 5 euros (cost for your Bulgarian bank receiving the funds, assuming 1 euro charge for every 1,000 euros). This will generally be charged by your Bulgarian bank of whichever service you use to send the funds.

3. 0 euros charge for sending the payment from your bank to XETrade (assuming that you use the internet to transfer the funds via BACS)

So a total of 17 euros.

If you were to ask your bank to transfer the funds, they would typically charge £23 for a CHAPS transfer in the UK, but you may still have the cost of receiving the money in Bulgaria to add to that.

You do need to be aware that UK banks do limit bank transfers on the internet via BACS, which can be anywhere between a daily limit of £2,000 –£10,000. Therefore, I advise you to contact your bank to determine what the maximum daily transfer amount is.

Alternative ways of transferring the money include:

1. Finding a foreign exchange currency company who you can purchase a euro rate from, and can then transfer the money for you

2. Sending the money directly between your own bank account and your Bulgarian bank account. This is typically the most expensive option

With some foreign currency exchange companies (including XETrade) you also have the option of putting in a bid and a bid expiry date. So you can effectively state the rate that you want, and as soon as that rate becomes available, it will be secured for you. For such a bid, you do need to declare the amount you want to purchase in advance, and must define a date by which you want to close the bid. If you do place a bid, you should always ensure that you have the funds available to pay for it.

There are currently no restrictions on the import or export of monies to and from Bulgarian bank accounts. This is obviously subject to change and you must check with your Bulgarian bank or solicitor for the latest situation.

MANAGING THE EVER-CHANGING EXCHANGE RATE

One thing is for certain. Foreign currency can be a volatile market, and one that sees a rapid frequency of change, virtually each second.

A good place to keep an eye on the exchange rate fluctuations is the Business and Money page of the BBC's website:

http://newsvote.bbc.co.uk/2/shared/fds/hi/business/market_data/overview/default.stm

To view the current rate of exchange in more detail you can click on the currency you are interested in to see more detail.

Currencies	£	$	€
£	–	1.8454	1.4928
$	0.5419	–	0.8088
€	0.6701	1.2364	–

Here, you will see a graph like the following:

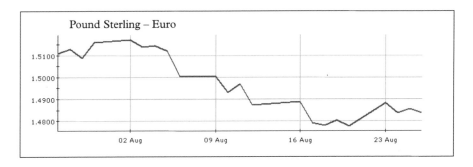

This will show you how the rate has varied over the period you have selected. You have the following choices:

1. One month

2. Three months

3. Twelve months

4. Intra day

Perhaps the most useful rate to track, if you are going to buy today, is the intra day rate. This shows the fluctuations of the currency over the course of the day. It allows you to see whether the rate is either on an up trend or a down trend. As you are likely to be buying your property in euros, you want to get as high a rate as you possibly can for your purchase. That means you should ideally aim to buy on an up trend.

Note that the exchange rate shown on the BBC website is a mid rate, and the actual rate you would get from your broker would typically be about 60-80 points lower than this rate. So, if the published rate on the website was 1.4880, you would typically expect to get about 1.480 from your broker. This does vary, but this provides you with an approximate indication of what to expect.

Sometimes, though, you want to have peace of mind, and if you want to secure a rate, you can buy a future rate with a currency exchange company. You will get a slightly lower rate, but would usually have the option to settle within 30 days.

Let's look at an example. Assuming that you want to buy at the rate of 1.48 – when the published rate is currently 1.486 – you can call your broker at the currency exchange company and request a future buy of the euro. They will offer you a rate – and assuming you get the 1.48 or above – you can secure this with them.

So, even if the rate drops over the next 30 days, you will still have secured the rate of 1.48. Naturally, this works both ways, so the down side is that if the rate improves, you lose out on the improved rate of exchange. If you are either running a tight budget or don't have all the money that you want to transfer yet, this is the recommended route.

So, yes, the rate can go up and down like a yo-yo, but there are steps you can take to avoid losing out. The key is to keep a constant watch on the rate of exchange and be aware of the trends. Try to buy on an up trend, and use the three or twelve month view of the graph to see whether it's likely to continue on a downward trend. There are no guarantees and you can only use your powers of intuition, knowledge of what's happening in the world economy and simple interrogation of the exchange rate graphs to try and predict whether the rate is going to grow any higher – or, ultimately – start its bear[9] run.

---

[9] For those of you unfamiliar with the term 'bear run' it generally refers to the consistent decline of the rate and is commonly used to describe a down trend on the stock market. Here, it refers to the decline of the exchange rate.

12

Living in or visiting your property

After all the hard work purchasing and furnishing your home, you are probably ready for a well deserved break. What better place than your dream home!

If you do leave your property vacant for any significant period, it would be wise to appoint keyholders who can open the windows from time to time, and perform any maintenance required. That way, you and your guests can be free from any irritating problems on your trips.

SECURITY

You should also consider installing a security system and smoke alarms, for additional safety. You can typically expect to pay on average about 500 euros for a security system, and fire detector (including installation).

When purchasing a security system, do consider the various options:

◆ Paying a monthly fee to a local security company, so that when the alarm is activated, the company calls you (or your representative) – which can cost upwards of 10 Leva/month

◆ Paying a monthly fee to a security company who will come to the property when the alarm is activated to investigate the problem – which can cost upwards of 20 Leva/month

◆ Just having an alarm bell, so that when the alarm rings it informs the neighbours!

INSTALLING CABLE OR SATELLITE TV

With a limited number of terrestrial television channels, and all of them in Bulgarian, you will almost certainly want to install cable TV or satellite.

Cable TV

The cost for installing cable TV (with MSAT, in Varna) ranges from between 40-50 Leva. The most common service is provided by MSAT which includes the following 'free-to-air' English speaking channels:

◆ CNN

◆ Cartoon network

◆ EuroNews

◆ EuroSport

◆ Hallmark

◆ MTV

◆ VH1

◆ Airrang

◆ Discovery

◆ Animal Planet

Sadly, at the time of writing, UK channels such as BBC 1, BBC 2, BBC World, ITV etc. are not available on the MSAT service. Whilst the BBC Prime channel is available in some parts of Europe on cable TV, this channel is also unavailable on the MSAT service at the time of writing.

The MSAT cable service also includes a number of Russian, German, French and Spanish speaking channels – ideal if you are planning to rent your Bulgarian property out to holidaymakers.

If you opt for cable TV, then you need to budget for an extra 11-13 Leva a month (this may vary depending on which company you use and where you are in the country). If you are renting your property out, it would be an idea to consider installing cable to provide your guests with some alternative foreign speaking channels during their stay. If you are looking for a wider variety of programmes, then you may wish to consider installing satellite instead.

Satellite TV

If you wish to view channels such as BBC 1, BBC 2 etc., you will need access to the Astra 2D satellite on 28.2°E. The BBC channels are free-to-air, which basically means that they are not encrypted.

Unfortunately, Bulgaria falls outside the natural footprint of this 2D beam. This means that the signal strength in Bulgaria is likely to be very weak. However, with a much larger dish of 4.5m, for example, in theory you should be able to pick up the BBC channels. I have yet to meet anyone who has tested this theory, but examination of the Astra 2D footprint and information that I have received from satellite engineers would suggest that it is at least feasible. Note that UK channels such as ITV, Channel 4 and Channel 5 are also available on Astra 2D but are not broadcast on free-to-air channels – i.e. they are encrypted.

As an expatriate planning to live in Bulgaria, you may wish to have access to the Astra 2AB satellite on 28.2°E. Although officially Astra's list of supported countries (within the Astra footprint) does not cover Bulgaria, it is possible to pick up the Astra channels as a satellite engineer in Bulgaria will verify. Sky programmes, amongst others, are broadcast from the Astra 2AB satellite, for example.

When enquiring about access to satellites in Bulgaria, a package that may be recommended is access to either or both:

♦ Hotbird 1 – 6 on 13°E

♦ Astra 2AB on 28.2°E

An engineer will generally advise you to purchase a satellite dish of between at least 1.2m-1.5m, in order to be able to receive the signal from Astra 2AB. For access to just the Hotbird satellite a 0.6m dish should suffice.

BBC Prime

If you want to access BBC Prime then you will need to subscribe to receive this channel from the BBC. At the time of writing this costs £85 (from the UK).

You will need to purchase a satellite receiver that supports the Viaccess encryption. This can be achieved by purchasing a receiver that supports a Common Interface (CI). This is a slot that enables a Conditional Access Module (CAM) to be inserted so that you can watch PAY-TV packages.

You can typically pay £65 for a Viaccess CAM and after paying the subscription to BBC Prime, you will be provided with a viewing card for a year that will fit into the CAM. Here, you will have an annual renewal for the BBC Prime subscription, but at least you will have a way of watching some of the popular BBC programmes whilst in Bulgaria.

Your satellite equipment must be compatible with the following specification:

Satellite:	Eutelsat Hotbird 6 – 13°East
Frequency:	11131 MHz
Antenna Configuration Name:	1 Hotbird
Polarisation:	Vertical
Beam:	Wide Beam
FEC:	3/4
Symbol Rate:	5.632
Conditional Access:	Viaccess

Satellite TV costs

The cost of installing satellite (including the receiver, dish etc.) can vary from as little as 200 Leva through to just under 400 Leva, on average. You should consider the programmes that you wish to receive, as these will dictate to some extent the size of dish that you buy, the type of receiver and ultimately the overall cost.

For a package that supports a 1.5m satellite dish and equipment supporting access to the Astra 2AB and Hotbird satellites, you would be typically looking to pay a one-off payment of between 370 and 400 Leva.

If you are looking for a cheaper package (just Hotbird, for example), with access to 200+ channels, including BBC World, for example, then you are looking to pay approximately 299 Leva, with a dish size of 0.6m. Going for a package with only FTA (free-to-air) channels means that you will have NO monthly bills, so for between 200 and 400 Leva you have all your costs covered.

You should always seek professional advice from a qualified satellite engineer and also ensure that you have checked on the legal issues around your viewing. For example, due to copyright restrictions, Sky's services and viewing cards can only be made available in the United Kingdom and Eire.

Whilst you may have heard that you can view Sky channels in Bulgaria – technically this is possible, but taking your Sky digibox and viewing card (under a subscription contract) from the UK to Bulgaria would be in breach of your contract with Sky. This means that Sky do have the right to block your viewing card, preventing you from accessing their channels.

Please refer to Appendix H for some useful websites that provide more information on satellite and cable access in Bulgaria.

INSTALLING AN INTERNET CONNECTION

Many of the 'internet service providers' in Bulgaria provide internet access via dial-up, cable or ISDN. The cost can vary considerably depending on the connection speed that you require. Broadband internet connection is still quite expensive in Bulgaria compared to Western Europe and North America. So the price that you may pay in England for a 512kbps connection, for example, may only allow you to get a 128kps/256kbps connection in Bulgaria for the same monthly fee.

The cost for installing cable internet is anywhere between 20–100 Leva, with monthly costs varying from 26–50 Leva a month (for a low end connection of 256 kbps) up to 116 Leva a month for a higher end connection of 2Mbps.

Dial-up internet access is by far the cheapest option, starting with free dial up – paying only for the minutes you use, on a standard 56kbps connection.

A growing number of providers are also making ADSL available for internet connections. For example, the Bulgarian Telecom Company (BTC) provides a service that uses ADSL – which (at the time of writing) delivers a 2Mbps broadband connection for 47.99 Leva per month (12 month contract). The installation fee is 36 Leva.

You will have to check whether the service is either limited (i.e. limited to a specific number of Gigabytes) or unlimited. There are surcharges to pay on those limited services when you exceed the maximum number of Gigabytes; so if you are likely to be transferring large amounts of data over the internet or cannot predict how much data you will transfer, the unlimited option may be more cost effective.

MOVING TO BULGARIA

You may be one of the growing number of people who are looking to retire in Bulgaria – or may be looking to spend some time working there perhaps. To do this you will need to assess the visa situation.

Before Bulgaria joined the EU in 2007, British citizens (and other EU citizens) required a Type 'D' visa, which covered the first three months in Bulgaria – before applying for a long term resident permit ('lichna carta') for a longer stay. This situation has changed –so EU citizens no longer have to apply for a Type 'D' visa.

What this means is that any EU citizen can enter Bulgaria for up to three months with just their passport or ID card. Beyond that, you would have to apply for a long stay permit (see later section 'long term resident permit').

For those of you who do not belong to an EU country, you will still require a Type 'D' visa and should read on.

Type 'D' visa

For longer-term stays for the purpose of business and/or residency a Type 'D' visa is required – it is obtainable from the nearest Bulgarian embassy, usually in the country of nationality. The application for a type 'D' visa can be applied for at your local Bulgarian embassy. The processing time varies, and can be anywhere from one to three months and above. The type 'D' visa itself will cover you for a period of up to 90 days.

The supporting documents that you require will depend on the reason for your application, which would generally fall under these categories:

◆ Business

◆ Foreign investment

◆ Private (retirement for example)

Purpose of stay for the type 'D' visa application

The purpose of stay for the type 'D' visa application will depend upon your circumstances. If you are retiring in Bulgaria, then the private option (for retirement) would be the most suitable, with some means of proof that you are retiring or have retired already.

The foreign investment route may be more appropriate for you if you have purchased property in Bulgaria and have obtained the necessary notary deed(s) as proof of your investment. The application form itself does not have an explicit category for 'foreign investor' and there are no specific guidelines as to which category you should complete for this option, so completing the 'Other' option with 'foreign investor' may be your best course of action.

If you are planning to work in Bulgaria or have set up your own Bulgarian company then you would be advised to apply under the 'business' category.

You should discuss this with your solicitor in Bulgaria to determine the most appropriate form of application. Your solicitor may also provide a service in which they prepare the paperwork for you, in order to submit the type 'D' application. Do note though, that at the time of writing, you still have to submit these papers yourself at the embassy. Your solicitor in Bulgaria **cannot** do this for you.

If you do not have one of the documents required, then you should be informed that you can post the remaining documents to the embassy when you receive them. The embassy should provide you with a receipt for your application (which has a number on it). You will be informed of the expected date on which you can collect your type 'D' visa.

Long-term resident permit

From January 1st 2007, the long term resident permit, referred to locally as a 'lichna carta' (personal ID card), has been renamed 'certificate for a long term stay'. To apply for this certificate the applicant must fulfil one of the following conditions:

◆ the applicant is an employee or is self-employed

◆ the applicant has the necessary funds to maintain their stay in Bulgaria

◆ the applicant is studying in a Bulgarian school and has the necessary funds to sustain their stay in Bulgaria

The application form must be submitted to the Ministry of Internal Affairs (typically attached to the police stations) within three months of entering Bulgaria.

Other documents that must be submitted with your application include:

◆ Copy of passport

◆ Documents proving the legal grounds for the application (which can be prepared by a solicitor, to make it easier for you) – e.g. property notary deed

◆ Documents proving that you have paid any relevant state taxes

◆ Bank statements showing proof of financial funds

This new long term stay certificate is valid for up to a maximum of five years. However, the actual term that will be issued cannot be guaranteed. The applicant can request the full five year term, but may receive a different term. At the time of writing, typical cases grant between a three to five year stay. The longer the validity period of your passport, the more likelihood there is of you being granted a five year certificate.

Under the new law, this long term stay certificate is supposed to be issued on the same day of the application. In practice, at the time of writing, this process can still take up to one week to process.

Unlike the previous 'long term stay' permit, there is nominal 10 Leva fee for the application. However, at the time of submitting your application you have to complete a declaration to agree to pay a revised amount, should the Bulgarian government decide to increase this in the future! Governments, eh!

On a practical note, the new long term stay certificate does not contain a photograph (unlike the old long term stay permit) and also does not present a personal identification (EGN) number. This means that you should carry your passport for any situations where you need to prove your identity (e.g. in banks, notaries, contract signings etc). This is a major oversight on behalf of the Bulgarian government and only time will tell if this is remedied.

13

Renting out your property

It is fair to say that the rental market in Bulgaria is currently still in its infancy. Obviously there are properties available for rental, particularly in the major cities, but the market itself is relatively immature.

In the capital, Sofia, you are likely to find more companies that provide property management services – but even these companies are still in the early stages of development – and many would say, some way off the standards we have come to expect in Western Europe, North America etc.

DETERMINING THE RENTAL MARKET

If you intend to rent your home out then you should conduct some research into the rental market within your area.

You also need to decide what type of rental you want to provide:

◆ Short-term rental (targeting holidaymakers, for example)

◆ Medium-term rental (6 month – 1 year lets, for businessmen)

◆ Long-term rental (for locals, long-term business lets etc.)

When planning to rent out your property, it's a good idea to consider whether you are aiming for a short, medium or long-term rental market. If, for example, you plan to stay in your property for several months a year, it would be more sensible to aim for the short-term rental market – perhaps in the summer season.

If you only plan to stay between 1 week and 4 weeks in a year yourself, then you may be better advised to consider short to medium-term rentals.

Assuming you may have purchased solely for investment, you may opt for a secure monthly income and therefore aim towards a long-term rental; perhaps yearly rentals with an option to renew. The clear benefit of a longer-term rental is the security it provides you with for a guaranteed income.

A long-term rental would almost always have a fixed monthly rental for the term – which needs to reflect the type of property, the amenities, the location and the quality of the property. One potential drawback of a long-term rental is that the monthly incomes, whilst more secure, tend to be lower than short-term rentals. You also need to think about who is going to rent your property long-term. Within Bulgaria, a large proportion of people own their homes, so the concept of local people renting properties is not as high as you may find in other parts of Europe. Therefore, take some time to research the kind of people you are likely to attract.

Based within a few miles radius of Sofia's city centre it may be easy to attract foreign businessmen who want to be within easy travelling distance of their place of work. It may also be more reasonable to expect a higher monthly rental if you are marketing to foreign clients. If, on the other hand, you have opted for the short-term rental market, you are probably focussing more on tourists.

TARGETING HOLIDAYMAKERS

With the predicted increase in tourism, there really shouldn't be a shortage of holidaymakers willing to rent your home during the summer months (for short-term rentals).

Clearly, choosing a property in the right location for holidaymakers is an important part of your selection criteria.

As perhaps up to 70 per cent of tourists flock to the Black Sea Coast, a 'room with a view', so to speak, should provide a stable income during the summer months (from May to September).

One of the main advantages of renting your property out to tourists is that you are likely to receive a higher rental income when you look at it from the point of view of the weekly rate.

For example, where you may receive a weekly income of 295 euros from tourists – you may, in comparison, only receive 75 euros a week if it was let out on a long-term rental (e.g. to a local businessman).

Of course, one of the potential disadvantages of short-term rentals to holidaymakers is that there is likely to be a longer period of vacancy. With a longer period of vacancy (for example, during the winter months) you must consider the security on your property etc.

PROPERTY MANAGEMENT COMPANIES

When it comes to renting out your home, there are many factors to consider. First of all, do you want to use a company that provides a rental management service?

If you do, then you need to start reviewing the available suppliers of these services. Where possible, look for recommendations from people who have bought property in Bulgaria.

A small number of internet-based forums of like-minded individuals have been growing over the past year or so, and allow you to share the experiences of others. You may find this a useful source for recommendations.

Many of the estate agents in Bulgaria provide some form of rental management service. I have been quoted up to 25 per cent for such a service. Since the majority of estate agents cater more for medium/long-term rental, this is unlikely to suit you if you are only targeting holidaymakers.

Property management costs

You can expect to pay between 8-20 per cent for the rental management service, depending on the service you expect and the company who is providing the service – and 15 per cent would seem to be the average. You can of course negotiate the price – and if that fails, you can always go somewhere else!

Summary of property management services

Having established that you will require your property to be looked after, and a company who can find clients, etc., you also need to consider all the other services that you may require from this company.

Services for short-term rental (to holidaymakers)

1. Advertising your property (e.g. on the internet)

2. Taking payments from your tenants

3. Sending the payments to you (or depositing them in a local bank, safety deposit box etc.)

4. Arranging a pickup service from the airport for your guests

5. Organising police registration for non-EU foreign guests (a requirement under Bulgarian law)

6. Appointing a local keyholder to let your guests into the property and provide them with keys during their stay

7. Possibly providing welcome drinks, ensuring that your property has drinks available and supplies (coffee, tea, sugar etc.)

8. Providing cleaning services to ensure that the accommodation has been cleaned for your guests and has new bed linen for example

9. Spot checks on the property during the vacant period, to ensure its safety etc.

10. Providing you with monthly accounts that indicate income and expenditure

Services for medium/long-term rental

1. Appointing a local keyholder

2. Cleaning the property before/after each tenant

3. Taking payments from your tenants

4. Sending the payments to you (or depositing them in a local bank, safety deposit box etc.)

Do you need a property management service?

However you look at it, if you are not planning to live in Bulgaria permanently, then you will require some local assistance. The real decision is whether to use a professional company to manage it for you, someone local that you either know (and trust), or someone that has been recommended to you.

Whilst I have not heard of any bad experiences – in all likelihood, with the increased interest in the country from foreign investors, there will be sharks out there. And sharks bite, so make sure you have your wits about you. If you are looking for a property management company, do ask for references. If possible ask the property management company if you can contact both the owners and the tenants of properties that they manage to get a better feel for the way they conduct their business.

At the end of the day, you have to feel comfortable with the people you are dealing with. Trust takes time to develop, wherever you are in the world – so my advice would be to put your trust in someone you know, or someone that comes highly recommended.

Do be wary of any company that claims to guarantee a rental income – as it's virtually impossible to guarantee, unless of course the agency is prepared to fix the payments contractually, and pay you the guaranteed amount directly themselves for a stated period.

Over the next few years, as the Bulgarian real estate market matures, more and more companies will spring up and more comprehensive property management services will be available – competition will increase – just as it's done in Italy and Spain, and inevitably with greater choice comes more competitive pricing.

It doesn't take a rocket scientist to understand that trends in real estate do follow patterns – hence the predictions that Bulgaria will follow the same kind of growth in real estate prices as other parts of Europe have over the last 20 years. So, let's assume that you have found someone you trust (whether it is an individual or a company) – you now need to think about the pricing.

DETERMINING THE RENTAL PRICE

First of all take stock of your reasons for renting out the property. Think about how often you may want to stay there yourself, and establish whether you want a short, medium or long-term rental.

When deciding how much to rent out your property for it can help to talk to the local estate agents, any Bulgarian friends that you have (or have recently made!) and also use resources such as the internet to gauge the general prices for rental in your area.

The factors that will influence the price that you charge include:

♦ The market that you are targeting (short, medium or long-term)

♦ The market rental price for a property of a similar type in your area

♦ The costs that you incur for making your property available for rent (e.g. rental management costs, cleaning, laundry etc.)

♦ The location of the property

♦ The quality of the property (i.e. whether it is an economy, standard or luxury property)

♦ The amenities within the property (e.g. whether it includes cable TV, satellite, swimming pool etc.)

♦ The season (if you are targeting the short-term market)

For short-term rentals, the season really has to be considered in the pricing – as you wouldn't generally expect to get the same rental income in winter as you would in summer, especially in the coastal areas.

Do think about your costs when considering what to charge. On short-term rentals (and probably medium-term), you may include the electricity and water within the rental price – so you need to calculate what you would expect these costs to come to for the different seasons. Ask other people that are renting out a similar property, or perhaps discuss this with the local estate agents or your neighbours. Ask a range of people so that you have a more balanced view and are in a better position to make an informed decision. If you plan to make a TV available, factor in your monthly charges for cable TV (for example). In winter, it's likely that the heating bills will be higher, so be comfortable that the amount that you are charging will cover these costs and also continue to provide you with a reasonable profit.

Another consideration for short-term rentals is the provision for a 'damage' deposit – which you should ideally request on receipt of the final payment. This will cover the cost of any accidental damage caused by your short-term tenants, and would typically be of the order of 25% of the weekly rental, for each week that the client books. So, if the client is paying £300 a week, then charge a £75 damage deposit for each one week period. It is, of course, completely up to you what you charge – but in order to avoid scaring the clients away, do consider a reasonable amount. Also make it clear that the damage deposit is refundable.

HOW TO RECEIVE PAYMENTS FOR SHORT-TERM RENTALS

If you are renting out your property on a short-term basis, you will need to have a system that allows you to collect payments on a higher frequency. The average period for holidaymakers in the summer season is likely to be weekly.

I would recommend that you look at the payments in three parts:

1. Deposit

2. Final payment

3. Damage deposit

You can typically expect to request the deposit at the time of booking, to secure the apartment for the desired date. For the final payment and damage deposit, you may consider requesting that the client settle the balance within 4-8 weeks of departure.

If you are taking a last-minute booking, you may request full payment up front.

How clients should pay you

If you are based in the UK and are taking bookings in the UK then you will probably want to receive your payments in pounds sterling.

You may also be taking bookings from overseas. In this case, to avoid the charges normally associated with transferring money from one international bank to another, you may wish to arrange for the client to send the money by bank transfer to your Bulgarian bank account.

Assuming that you are catering to a European market then it may be wise to transfer the money to a Euro account in Bulgaria, to make it easier and more convenient for your clients. You could also consider opening a US dollar account, to make it more convenient for those who prefer US dollars. When dealing with multiple currencies, though, you do need to be aware of the currency conversion rates and how these may affect your overall profit, due to currency fluctuations.

For example, if you had been receiving payment in US dollars over the past year or so, the dollar's weakness against the pound would have made a dent in your profits. So do consider the currencies that you want to deal with carefully.

If you are using a property management company, then of course you can opt to leave the money collection to them, and arrange for the company to transfer money to your Bulgarian bank account on a monthly basis. A local property management company would be able to collect cash payment from the clients – which may be more comfortable to some people. You may consider using a combination, and take the UK bookings yourself and use a property management company to collect payments from other clients directly.

HOW TO ADVERTISE YOUR PROPERTY FOR RENTAL

There are a number of approaches that you can take to advertise your property. Here are the most common:

1. Use a property management company, who can advertise your property on their website.

2. Advertise your property for rental with one of the local estate agents in Bulgaria. A number of these estate agents also provide rental services.

3. Find an internet-based website that allows you to advertise your own property. There are several websites that provide this kind of service – see Appendix H for a selection of these.

4. Design your own website and employ the services of a web designer to build it for you. You can then buy your own website and take full control of the site.

5. Advertise in newspapers, noticeboards etc.

6. Word of mouth! This is by far the cheapest form of advertising there is. Talk to family and friends – you would be surprised how many people would jump at the chance to holiday in Bulgaria, as a refreshing change.

Advertising your property

In order to attract clients to your property it is important to think like one of your potential clients. What would you look for if you were renting a property?

In Bulgaria, private rental accommodation amongst foreign tourists is quite popular, particularly on the Black Sea Coast. However, when you view the various internet websites, you will not find hundreds of properties available for rent. This suggests that more traditional forms of advertising are currently more common (e.g. word of mouth, magazines and newspapers). The number of properties advertised on the internet for rental in Bulgaria is growing and you need to take into account the increasing competition.

Regardless of what media you are using to advertise your property, there are some basic points that you should follow:

◆ Photograph(s) that clearly show the property, preferably with interior and exterior views

◆ An indication of the number of bedrooms and other rooms in the property

◆ A list of the facilities within the property (e.g. TV, microwave, etc.)

- Its distance from the local attractions, city centre other amenities etc.

- Preferably a clear indication of the rental price

Advertising for the holiday rental market

Besides the above general points, you must also consider the fact that most people will generally need to have a clear indication of how many people the property sleeps. If you have a sofa bed, for example, then you can easily increase the number of people the property sleeps by another two (assuming it can convert into a double sofa bed).

Most holidaymakers choose their rental accommodation based on its distance from the local amenities – especially the beach and sea for coastal rentals; and the distance from the city centre for more urban areas. So do take the time to look around the local area and consider how you can best promote your property based on what is in the area.

What to include on a website

If you have decided to either use or build your own website, then here are a few ideas of what to include:

- Comprehensive details about the property, its rooms and facilities

- Photographs of the property

- Details of the local amenities

- Information about any local entertainment

- Details about some of the local restaurants

- Flight details, to assist overseas visitors who are travelling to Bulgaria

- Your contact details (email address, telephone number etc.)

- If applicable, the methods of payment you accept

- A calendar that shows the availability of the property

- The prices (per week, and per person per night if applicable)

Modern apartment building (Veliko Turnovo, North Central Bulgaria)

© WorldAtlas.com.

Sunny beach, South East Bulgaria

Nessebar, South East Bulgaria

Unique style of roof in the village of Kovachevitza, South West Bulgaria

Near Kardzhali, South East Bulgaria

Pamporovo

Ski lifts in Pamporovo, Smolyan district, South Central Bulgaria

Beautiful Pamporovo – premier ski resort in Bulgaria

The magnificent Opera House on Plaza Nezavisimost, central Varna.

Sofia

© Quest Bulgaria Magazine   © Quest Bulgaria Magazine

Ruse

© Quest Bulgaria Magazine   © Quest Bulgaria Magazine

Traditional Bulgarian architecture

Modern apartment complex, Varna sea garden

250 year old renovated house in Veliko Turnovo

Example of apartment interior

Bulgarian house in Melnik, South West Bulgaria

Tryavna, North Central Bulgaria

Beautiful Bulgaria

Dospat lake, close to the Greek border, Bulgaria

View over Yantra river, Veliko Turnovo (central Bulgaria)

Veloko Turnovo, old town

Rila Monastery, Rila mounains, 117km south of Sofia

Ralitza Ranguelova, a true Bulgarian artist in every sense, has been living in England now for the last five years. She regularly exhibits in the Aubergine gallery in Wimbledon and produces original paintings and commissions that reflect a unique, vibrant and inspiring style.

The two paintings on the next page reflect Ralitza's own interpretation of Bulgaria – in particular its landscape and coastal scenes, which I shall leave you with to enjoy.

Ralitza Ranguelova
Website: www.ralitza-art.com

'Sea Blessing' © Ralitza Ranguelova, 2004

'From the heart of my country' © Ralitza Ranguelova, 2004

◆ Transport details (how to get to your property and a rough indication of the price to get there)

◆ Local places of interest

COSTS ASSOCIATED WITH RENTING OUT YOUR PROPERTY

There are some costs that you must also consider when you are renting out your property, which include:

◆ Buildings and contents insurance

◆ Electricity and water

◆ Telephone

◆ Maintenance costs for serviced apartments

◆ Annual government tax on the property (approximately 0.15 per cent)

◆ Garbage collection costs

◆ Cable TV subscription

◆ Any repair work (following damage from tenants etc.)

◆ Keyholder/property management company costs

◆ Cleaning costs

◆ Advertising costs (if you are promoting your property on websites, or in magazines)

Some of these costs will be paid for by your tenants if you are renting on either a medium or long-term basis. However, if you are renting your property on a short-term basis, it is likely that you will be paying the majority of these costs directly.

POINTS TO CONSIDER WHEN RENTING OUT YOUR PROPERTY

Renting out your property really needs to be looked at as a 'business' in its own right, and managed in a similar way to managing a business. Consider the following points:

1. The rental market in your area

2. The rental season and price per season

3. The unique selling points of your property

4. Payment of ongoing costs (utilities, property tax, garbage collection, security etc.)

5. Payments to a property management company to look after and manage the property

6. Buildings and contents insurance

7. Advertising costs (e.g. websites usually charge an annual fee for advertising property for rental)

8. How your clients are going to pay (by cheque, bank transfer, in cash etc.)

9. What currencies you will accept payment in

RENTAL YIELDS

As an investor, or even as a home owner looking to rent out your property for part of the year, it is important to assess the likely returns that you can expect on your property.

A typical measure for this return is the gross yield, expressed as a percentage. This is defined as:

$$\text{Gross (rental) yield (\%)} = \frac{\text{Expected gross annual rental income} \times 100}{\text{Purchase price}}$$

From this simple equation it is quite obvious that your gross yield will depend on a number of factors, such as how much you paid for the property and how much you can obtain during the year from renting out your property.

The purchase of a luxury apartment in Varna, on the Black Sea Coast in 2008, costing 130,000 euros could receive an annual rental income of 11,400 euros. This would represent a gross rental yield of 8.7 per cent and assumes a long term rent, based on 950 euros a month.

At the beginning of 2008, the average UK rental yield was reported to be 5.72 per cent. The ability to achieve a rental yield of 8.7 per cent or more would therefore be considered very good.

In the capital city, Sofia, you can typically expect to receive a gross yield of between 8–12 per cent.

14

Investing in Bulgaria

In the first edition of this book I reported an 18 per cent growth in property prices for 2003. The Bulgarian National Statistics Institute have published statistics that show the average price of an apartment in Bulgaria has increased as illustrated in the table below:

Year	Average apartment price (Leva/m^2)
2004	540.5
2005	738
2006	846.5
2007	1091.2

Comparing the average price of an apartment between 2004 and 2007, this represents an increase of over 102% on the 2004 price. Whilst property prices are expected to increase at a slower pace over 2008/2009, they are still expected to provide an excellent return on investment for the medium to long term, assuming you choose your property wisely.

The Black Sea Property Fund (launched by Development Capital Management in 2005) alone is investing 50 million pounds in Bulgarian real estate. Looking at current economic indicators – such as the GDP growth at 5.7 per cent (in 2006), Bulgaria continues to offer a good climate for investment.

A number of countries have been investing in Bulgaria, including:

◆ United Kingdom

◆ Germany

◆ Turkey

◆ USA

◆ Switzerland

◆ Netherlands

◆ France

◆ Cyprus

◆ Greece

MAJOR INVESTMENT INCENTIVES

◆ Corporate tax rate – 10 per cent (reduced in January 2007 from 15% to 10%) and 0% in areas of high unemployment

◆ Annual depreciation rate of 30 per cent for machinery and equipment and 50 per cent for software and hardware

◆ Opportunity to buy land through a company registered in Bulgaria with up to 100 per cent foreign ownership

◆ Adoption of International Accounting Standards

◆ 52 treaties for avoidance of double taxation

◆ 49 agreements on mutual protection and promotion of foreign investment

As far as the legal framework is concerned in Bulgaria the right of ownership is guaranteed by law. However, land cannot be owned directly by a foreigner. That is why it is necessary to set up a corporate structure for the purchase of property / land. Let's take a look at some of the international investors in Bulgaria:

◆ American Standards – largest European sanitary houseware production facility

◆ Solvay (Belgium) – fully integrated chemical plant

◆ Unicredito Italiano Group – successful privatisation of the Bulgarian Foreign Trade Bank (Bulbank)

◆ ABB – power generation equipment in the energy hub of South Eastern Europe

◆ SKF – low-cost bearings production and assembly

The following British based companies have also been investing in Bulgaria:

◆ Shell

◆ Shell Gas

◆ Cable and Wireless

◆ Regent Pacific Group

◆ Rio Tinto

◆ United Utilities

◆ Petreco Sarl

As for the investment in the telecom infrastructure, according to an article published on the Novinite.com website in May 2004:

'Vienna-based Viva Ventures will invest 700 million euros in the upgrade and improvement of Bulgaria's telecom infrastructure to offer high-quality service to its clients and give access of other operators to its network. The company expressed the belief that the deal will serve as an incentive for competition among the players on the market of telecommunications services.'

BRITISH BULGARIAN CHAMBER OF COMMERCE

The British Bulgarian Chamber of Commerce (BBCC) was formed in 1993 in order to help promote and support business between the United Kingdom and Bulgaria. They host a number of events which include business missions, seminars and social meetings throughout the year.

In May 2004, the BBCC hosted a seminar called 'Practical guidance on buying property in Bulgaria' which was attended by some 175 participants. Such events are a great opportunity to learn more about the ins and outs of buying property in Bulgaria and give you the opportunity to meet with others who are also considering investment in Bulgaria's real estate.

You will also find that a number of the UK based agents that deal with property sales in Bulgaria are members of the chamber of commerce, as well as some of the local Bulgarian estate agents. To become a member, you can be either a British or Bulgarian company or an individual.

Membership class	Subscription rate
Corporate – large company (over £10m turnover)	£250
Corporate – medium size company (£5-10m turnover)	£200
Corporate – small size company (under £5m turnover)	£150
Non-corporate (private individual)	£100

To find out more about the business and investment opportunities in Bulgaria, contact the British Bulgarian Chamber of Commerce. Their website http://www.bbcc.bg provides a comprehensive list of all their members and is a useful point of reference for establishing new contacts and making business acquaintances. Their full contact details can be found in Appendix I.

15

Buying land in Bulgaria

Buying land in Bulgaria is definitely not for the faint-hearted. However, if you can get over the hurdles then it may well be worth its weight in gold in the future. We shall look at the hurdles later in this chapter – specifically the kind of things that can go wrong when you buy land, and some of the things to look out for.

Remarkably, the price of land is still very low in Bulgaria when compared to the rest of Europe. This is particularly true of plots located in rural areas where agricultural land can be found as low as 2 euro/sq m. At the extreme, prices of land in 2008 were reaching in excess of 300 euro/sq m in prime locations around Varna and districts like Boyana in Sofia.

Land prices have even increased by 100 per cent in some areas within the space of a year.

You have probably read property investment magazines that highlight the risks of buying anything in Eastern Europe – issues such as political stability, economic factors, the fact that they are still getting used to their independence from communism. But consider this. If you are successfully persuaded not to buy in Bulgaria, who do you think is going to invest there? The writers of these articles (and their friends) perhaps?

Any investment requires the assessment of risk and professional advice on legal issues. Having equipped yourself with some sound legal and financial advice, you are then in the best position to make your own choice. Always question the motives of those that try to put you off. Obviously, sometimes they are merely warning you of the risks, but sometimes there are other motives in play.

◆ **TOP TIP** ◆

Prices of land in Bulgaria are continuing to increase. For the medium/long term you should make land investment a part of your real estate portfolio. Prices have quadrupled in some regions between 2003 and 2008.

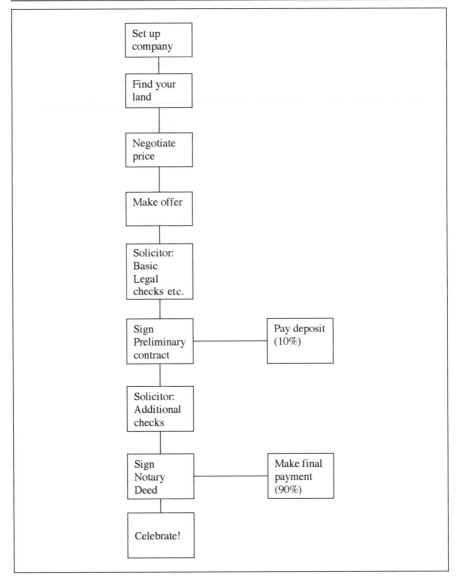

FIGURE 2 Steps to buying land in Bulgaria

REGULATED VERSUS UNREGULATED LAND

As you view plots of land in Bulgaria, you will sometimes find that the agent uses terms such as 'regulated' and 'unregulated' land.

If you are viewing unregulated land, then this typically means that the authorities have not marked that area for development. It does not mean that you cannot build there, but you would need to go through a legal process to convert the land to 'regulated' land. Regulated land, therefore, means that the land has been marked for development (e.g. building).

When viewing land it is important to establish whether the land is regulated or not, as this will determine how easily and how quickly you will be able to build a property on it. Some agents will tell you that they can help you to get the land regulated. However, it is always better to get independent advice on how easy a process this will be. I would suggest that you discuss this point with your solicitor to ensure that the whole legal process has been explained to you and you have been given a clear idea of how long this can take.

You will typically hear claims that regulation can take anywhere between one and six months. But there is really no 'official' length of time by which regulation of land can be obtained, and there is also no guarantee, as such, that unregulated land can be regulated.

The safest option for you would be to purchase regulated land. Ensure that you tie a clause in to your contract (with your solicitor's recommendation) that protects your interests on this point.

CAN A FOREIGNER BUY LAND IN BULGARIA?

Technically speaking, a foreign national cannot buy land on an individual basis at the time of writing. However, as with houses, it is possible to form a Bulgarian company and purchase the land under that company. The procedure is therefore almost identical to that of buying a house (with land).

You still go through the process of signing a preliminary contract first and then a final contract (the notary deed) to take legal ownership.

HOW DO YOU GO ABOUT BUYING LAND?

For some people, the prospect of buying land in a foreign country can be somewhat daunting. Even in one's own country, perhaps!

In Bulgaria, you can typically buy land from the same people that you go to to buy property. Whilst land plots are usually dealt with by different agents, you can easily approach any of the local agents and discuss your criteria with them, and probably be out of the door and on your way to the first plot within an hour. So, the easiest option is to go with an estate agent.

Alternatively, you could purchase one of the local property papers and attempt to contact land owners directly. In this case you will more than likely require the services of a local translator or a Bulgarian friend – at least to assist in locating the land plots you are interested in so that you can visit the plot.

IS IT EASY TO BUY LAND?

It is, in actual fact, remarkably easy to buy the land itself. That's not where the problems lie! You do require a Bulgarian company in order to purchase the land (which you may already have formed if you have already pur-chased a home in Bulgaria) – but if you haven't got a company, its quite straightforward to set up and the agent will usually be able to provide this service to you (see Chapter 4).

The problems are more often associated with the legal issues that may be lurking behind the land plots and issues that develop with the sellers before you have signed on the dotted line. I will explain this in more detail in the section *What can go wrong?*

BUYING LAND WITH AN AGENT

If buying land with an agent, it is likely that you will first be asked to sign a document in which you agree to the agent's terms. This is typically a com-mission of 3 per cent. As these terms may be presented to you in Bulgarian, it is well worth having a translator present to verify the contents of the terms and conditions.

If you feel that the commission is too high or unreasonable then bargain with the agent before you sign. As there is so much competition amongst real estate agents, it is quite easy to persuade them to discount their commission by at least a small margin.

WHAT ARE THE APPROXIMATE COSTS AND FEES ASSOCIATED WITH BUYING LAND?

The main costs / fees can be summarised as:

Estate agent commission	Approximately 3%
Legal fees (for lawyer)	Approximately 1%
Municipal tax, court fee and notary fees	Approximately 2.2% – 3.5%

Percentages are expressed in terms of the purchase price.

So you are looking at somewhere between 6-10 per cent in additional costs, on top of the price that you pay for the land.

WHAT CAN GO WRONG?

With land prices increasing all the time, it's not surprising that sellers want to maximise their profit. In some regions south of Varna, you can expect to pay well over 200 euros per square metre. Just north of Varna it is still possible to buy land in some areas (at the time of writing) from 15 euros per square metre and above.

Just when you thought you were about to become the proud owners of a plot of land, though, you may find a number of reasons why the deal falls through. Here are just a few reasons:

1. The date you agreed to sign the preliminary contract has passed (for whatever reason) and the seller has decided to increase the price of the plot by 50 per cent!

2. The land does not actually belong to the 'seller'. In fact, the seller has the 'right' to purchase the land from the government, but has not

actually done so yet. This is allegedly quite a common occurrence in Bulgaria. However, if your solicitor is strict, he/she may insist on certain documents being presented before the preliminary contract is signed. In this case, you may lose the deal because the seller does not want to wait to sign the preliminary contract before he/she has purchased the land from the government.

3. The seller decides at the last minute (before signing the preliminary contract) that he/she does not want to sell anymore.

4. The seller simply decides (for no apparent reason) to increase the price of the land, just before signing the preliminary contract – because he/she can!

5. The seller is not the exclusive owner of the land. In fact, the ownership is in several names. This can create some fantastically complicated situations that present great challenges to your solicitor!

6. The seller is advised by his sons / daughters not to sell the property, because he/she can probably charge more money.

Those of you that have experienced the joys of buying land in Bulgaria will more than likely be smiling when you read this, whilst others of you could probably add a few more reasons.

Whilst it is not my intention to put you off buying land in Bulgaria, I feel an obligation to make you aware of the potential problems that you may face so that you can be better prepared and in a better position to negotiate the deals.

WHAT SHOULD YOU WATCH OUT FOR?

When you have seen the plots with an agent, it is possible that you may be asked to give a deposit – even before the preliminary contract. However, you should not feel pressured into doing this.

It is normal to pay a 10 per cent deposit at the point of signing the preliminary contract but not to pay any other form of deposit before then. Basically, the agent is trying to secure their commission from you as soon as they can, and actually plan to use this money towards their commission.

Just beware. At the very least, offer 100 euros or so, but beware of departing with any more until you have reached the preliminary contract stage. Your solicitor is the best person to turn to for the right professional advice. A good solicitor will always try to protect your interests and will generally suggest that you don't part with any of your money until you have signed the preliminary contract.

There are stories of people who have paid out more and then the deal has fallen through and the deposit has not been returned.

Do appoint an independent solicitor to make the necessary legal checks. It is possible that there are ownership problems with the land – perhaps people who could claim inheritance on the land, or a mortgage on the land. All such matters require careful assessment by your solicitor.

If you are concerned about losing the land if the legal checks are likely to take some time, then you can consider adding sufficient clauses to the preliminary contract to protect your interests.

Other problems you may face with the land include landslide issues. There are certain designated 'red zones' known for landslide activity and you should make every effort to ensure that the plot you are buying is not in such a zone, and not subject to landslide activity. This can occur in some areas of the Black Sea Coast, and various articles available on the internet indicate the known areas for this activity.

Buying land by a cliff edge!

If you are buying a plot of land by the coast, particularly on a cliff edge, do check that it is not in a 'red zone' – this is best done by your solicitor. If you ask your agent, they are likely to tell you that everything is okay and their legal representative has already checked the papers.

This may of course be true, but don't take any chances as I can tell you from experience, this is not always the case – and you may be surprised what your own solicitor uncovers.

What is a 'first line' plot?

You will hear the terms 'first line', 'second line', 'third line' etc. when you are looking at plots of land close to the cliff edge. What these terms refer to is the distance from the cliff edge.

First line plots are the plots that quite literally go to the cliff edge, or within five metres or so of the cliff edge.

Many buyers want to buy the 'first line' plots, because they are obviously not going to suffer from any obstruction in the future. First line plots will therefore be higher in price, because they will be unobstructed and offer the best possible view of the coast.

Sometimes, however, you may find yourself being shown a 'first line' plot, when in actual fact it's a 'second line' plot. In this case, you must ensure that your solicitor checks all the paperwork to establish that the land is in a 'first line' position and that any land in front of the plot does not belong to someone else.

A tell-tale sign is when the price of the plot seems too good to be true. For example, if you view a plot of land in Topola (north of Varna) that claims to be 9,000 euros for 'first line', do ensure that it is, before you buy it. This is very important if you specifically want to buy a first line plot with unobstructed views.

Whilst it could still be the genuine price for a 'first line' plot in Topola, in 2008 'first line' plots cost anywhere between 65-90 euros per square metre. So, a typical 600 square metre plot would typically have cost you upwards of 39,000 euros or so.

BUILDING A HOUSE ON THE LAND

If you are planning to build a house on the plot of land you are buying, you need to be aware that different regions have different regulations on this. The local area municipality will generally assign a certain percentage of the land in which you are permitted to build a house. This can typically be anything from 20-50 per cent.

Bulgarians would typically look to buy a plot somewhere between 500-600 square metres. It's generally considered that a 600 metre square plot is the optimal size for building a villa. If you are looking to build a house, and have a plot of land in mind, it's a good idea to meet with an architect to check that you can build the size of house you want on that plot.

Engaging the services of an architect in Bulgaria can cost upwards of 15 euros per square metre based on the size of the property you plan to construct. Therefore, if you were to build a house of 130 square metres, you can expect the five stages of the architect's project (as outlined below) to cost upwards of 1,950 euros.

Initial study

The architect may recommend that an initial study is performed to determine any additional costs that may arise during the project. This will usually determine whether there are likely to be any additional costs due to:

◆ The electric supply company not having any power supply mains available to the plot

◆ No mains water pipeline to the plot. This may require you to connect your water pipeline to a private water supply, for example. If there is no sewer, then you will also have to consider the construction of a septic pit / tank.

◆ Additional considerations if the plot is in a known landslide area (e.g. costs associated with strengthening the foundations etc.)

To perform this initial study successfully, you should provide your architect with a basic scheme (plan) of the plot of land. You should have this when you purchased the plot of land – I suggest you check this with your solicitor. A plan is required for any further work that the architect will perform on the design and to look at the various options for the building construction etc.

The cost of such an initial study would be approximately 200 euros.

Site plan

If there is no detailed scheme (blueprint plan) developed for the plot of land, then it is necessary to develop such a plan before the project starts. You can typically expect to pay approximately 200 euros for this stage.

Stages in the architect's project

The architect will make a detailed plan which typically consists of the following stages:

Stage 1 – preliminary design

This design covers several versions of the house designs for you to make your choice. This design can be typically presented in 3D model. The time required for the development of the preliminary design would be typically 20 days.

Stage 2 – working design

The working design shall be made in scale 1:50. The time required for the development of the working design covering all parts of the project would be typically 30 days. The time needed for the approval of the design documentation would be approximately 45 days.

Stage 3 – design of water supply and sewerage

This part of the project deals with all the pipe-work and installation of the house water supply and sewerage system.

Stage 4 – design of the electrical supply

This part of the design of the house covers the electric installation, including thunder protection. However, this section of the project does not include security alarm systems.

Stage 5 – construction design

The construction design deals with the construction works. This should be checked by the Municipality responsible for the area where the property will be located.

In 2008, the average price of the building work was approximately 400–500 euros per square metre. The actual price will usually be indicated in the offer made by the construction company on the basis of a completed *working design* as per the various parts of the Project – architectural, constructional and the *bill of quantities*. Obviously the building cost depends on the quality of materials used.

Additional costs to consider

◆ Geological Survey (~ 100 euros)

◆ Tacheometrical Survey (~ 100 euros)

◆ Garden Layout (~ 200 euros)

◆ Interior Design (~ 4 euros per sq.m)

◆ Bill of Quantities (~ 0.5 euros per sq.m)

◆ Approval of the project performance time and state charges (~ 200 euros)

◆ Architect's supervision of the project (~ 5 euros per hour)

◆ Manager's fee for managing the project (~ 15 euros per sq.m)

It is essential that you employ the services of a project manager, unless you want to take this role on yourself! The manager must have the power to sign papers on your behalf, including the documents required for the design and for the building.

The same manager, or another person, could be appointed to supervise the design and the construction works as a whole, to hire designers and builders and to sign contracts.

Stages of payment for the architect's project

A typical payment profile is outlined below:

◆ 30 per cent at the beginning of the architectural design

◆ 30 per cent at the beginning of the working design

◆ 40 per cent at finalization of the project

Construction

The timescale for building a house in Bulgaria depends on several factors. This includes:

◆ The availability of finance for the various stages in the project

◆ The quality and reliability of the builders that you use

◆ The type and size of the property that you are building

Typically, you can expect the timescale for the build to be anywhere from four to eight months.

HOW DO I FIND PEOPLE TO BUILD MY PROPERTY?

There are some companies based in the UK that are providing a service to build homes in Bulgaria.

To build the home itself, you may be looking at an all-in cost of between 52,000 euros and 150,000 euros (including kitchen and bathroom). This will always depend on the quality of fixtures and fittings, and this excludes the cost of furnishing the house.

If you want to deal with construction companies in Bulgaria, then you can contact any estate agent to provide you with details of architects, builders etc. – and a number of these agents also provide the ability to build homes for you.

Building a home yourself, despite the end rewards, can be a very stressful and time consuming-process – and perhaps even more taxing in a foreign country where many of the local procedures may not be known.

You could opt to use a company to build a home to your specifications. Such companies would typically expect the payments for the various stages to be profiled as follows:

Initial deposit to start the project	30%
Deposit to secure the land	10%
Completion of building stage one	30%
Final completion of building	30%

16

Inside the mind of the Bulgarian

In order to be successful with the purchase of your property (or land) you need to understand how Bulgarians think. In this chapter I hope to provide you with the 'upper hand' when you are dealing in Bulgaria by gaining an insight into the way that Bulgarians think – nearly all the information in this chapter was freely provided to me by several Bulgarians that I know!

It is certainly not my intention to insult the Bulgarian people – amongst whom I have many friends and acquaintances – but more to relate some important traits that may assist you in negotiating deals and understanding the Bulgarian mentality.

1. Yes means no and no means yes! What I am actually referring to is the fact that the normal nodding gesture made in the West to denote 'yes' actually means 'no' in Bulgaria, and vice versa. This can of course be very confusing for both parties if unaware! Generally speaking, though, Bulgarians are aware of this difference – but do not assume that they have adjusted their nods and shakes.

2. Bulgarian villagers do not trust estate agents! In fact, they can be known to refuse to pay their 3 per cent commission. So who does pay this commission? You do. The buyer! I was faced with this very situation and the seller had no inhibitions about declaring that I was to pay the commission fee that they owed the agent! This is perhaps one of the hardest things to get used too, but it is common in some areas.

3. Bulgarians hate the taxman even more than the English! That's why you may find yourself in a sticky dilemma wanting a house or plot of

land, and faced with a seller who is insisting on declaring the **lower** price. Your solicitor will advise you on what to do in this situation.

4. Bulgarians, once they cotton on to a good thing, will copy it, and copy it, and copy it again!

    This is best explained by an example that was once passed on to me by an estate agent who told me a story about a particular village where a certain type of shop opened. Once the shop started to become successful, several other shops of the same type opened up. And this is an allegedly common trait, so I am told.

5. Bulgarians believe that you should not lend money on a Monday! Since it is the beginning of the week, it is believed to be a sign for the week ahead – and one to avoid!

6. Bulgarians are very hospitable people who would always take you in and are very tolerant towards foreign people.

7. When buying flowers, always buy an odd number of flowers. But for a funeral, an even number of flowers. So Bulgarians generally believe it's bad luck to buy an even number!

8. Bulgarians would generally have their house blessed by a priest before they live there. The last thing to go into the house must be earth! (i.e. a plant etc.)

9. If a Bulgarian leaves the house and forgets something, it is considered bad luck to go back and get it. On some occasions, they may turn around in a circle, and then return to get it!

10. It is considered a warm, welcoming gesture to present a gift to your Bulgarian hosts when you meet them. For example, chocolates, a bottle of wine or spirits.

11. Tipping in restaurants and taxis is considered normal. This would be normally rounding the bill up, for example. Typically this would be just a few Leva.

17

Bulgaria: the future

What does the future hold for Bulgaria? Economic reports, the consistent performance of the real estate market over the last few years and an increasing tourist trade are all strong economic pointers for a country that is going places.

If you also consider that Bulgaria is already a member of NATO and joined the European Union in 2007, the next few years would suggest a healthy growth within the country.

Take my advice, and book yourself on a flight there and take a look around for yourself. You do not have to believe all you read – whether it be good or bad – so be your own judge! If you venture Varna way, and look around those districts close to Golden Sands, you will find the whole infrastructure in development – with new roads, brand new petrol stations opening – all strong economic indicators of a developing nation.

Thomas Cook has set up a 100 million euros special fund for construction and refurbishment of its 15 hotels in Bulgaria. The company spent 17.5 million euros revamping nine hotels along the Black Sea Coast in 2002.

Resorts along the northern section of the Black Sea shore, including Golden Sands and Albena, have attracted most of the investment.

Sure, there is room for improvement, as can be said about practically every country in the world. Infrastructure in Bulgaria does need improving further – and in particular the roads – but funding from the EU is likely to address these issues within the next decade. As I have already stated, development of new roads has already started and can be easily seen on the road to Golden Sands from Varna. Here you will find smooth, tarmac roads, recently laid – that are dream to travel on.

Take a stop at one of the petrol stations on the way. What do you notice? It is spotlessly clean, it has a small area for eating cakes – sells drinks and provides an area where you can sit down and relax. Very civilised!

MY PREDICTION OF BULGARIA'S FUTURE

I would predict that well within the next decade Bulgaria will have established itself as a holiday destination that is on a par with Spain – as the country boasts mountains of culture, history, adventure, natural beauty, glorious coastlines and some of the kindest people you could ever want to meet.

Low-cost airlines

Low-cost airlines will start providing much more affordable flights to the region, with direct flights to Burgas and Varna. Both Wizz Air and Easyjet are already operating flights between London and Sofia, and you can fly from Burgas to London directly; and Varna to London via Budapest on Wizz Air.

Increase in tourism

Following the availability of low-cost flights (from the UK, for example) the number of tourists will increase – all helping the Bulgarian economy. This increased interest and availability of low-cost flights will have a knock-on effect on the price of properties in the country – particularly in the popular cities and coastal areas.

Increase in emigration to Bulgaria

You will find more and more foreign retirees moving out to Bulgaria over the course of the next few years – as a place to wind down in their twilight years. As its infrastructure improves and its services develop, more and more people will be attracted to live and work there.

Why? Because Bulgaria is a beautiful country, full of natural unspoilt beauty and perhaps some of the most stunning scenery one could encounter in Europe. Sure, the price of development will make its mark on the country and it will gradually reduce the number of unspoilt areas – but this will be carefully controlled by the government I am sure.

There are a growing number of foreigners emigrating to Bulgaria to start a new life out there. It's very affordable, with a low cost of living presently. Yes, prices will rise, but so will local opportunities for business and commerce. It's all set to follow the footsteps of other countries that were also undeveloped decades ago – but with time and investment, grew into more desirable locations.

Growth in services, such as information technology

Bulgaria has a highly respected information technology (IT) work force, whose cost is low compared to Western Europe and North America – and is currently amongst the lowest paid countries for services in IT.

The top ten countries with the most certified IT professionals are:

1. United States

2. India

3. Russian Federation

4. Ukraine

5. Canada

6. Romania

7. United Kingdom

8. **Bulgaria**

9. Pakistan

10. Australia

Source: Brainbench Inc., 2002.

Between 2001 and 2002 it is reported that there were more than 1,000 SME's (small to medium enterprises) in Bulgaria. It is also worth noting that Bulgarians rank second in IQ tests (Mensa international).

The upper annual salary for an IT specialist in Bulgaria is between 9,000-14,000 euros (gross) per annum. Salaries in the IT industry in the UK average £25,000 (37,500 euros) which is more than 300 per cent higher!

Whilst salaries will increase – there is a clear opportunity in the growing 'outsourcing' market to consider Bulgaria.

Companies with enough courage to wake up to this opportunity stand to gain an advantage in this highly competitive world that we live in.

Your part in Bulgaria's future
If every one of you reading this book visited Bulgaria to experience the land, the people, the property and ultimately bought your own home – then this influx of foreign investment would only add to the growth of the country as a whole. After all, anyone building a property in Bulgaria will employ local architects, builders, drivers etc.

So let's start welcoming Bulgaria into the EU!

18

Case study: Varna

VARNA: BACKGROUND

Varna, Bulgaria
Latitude: 43° 12' N
Longitude: 27° 55' E
Elevation: 35 m
Population: 350,000+

Situated 469 km north east of Sofia, Varna lies on the west coast of the Black Sea with a population of over 350,000 people and has a large industrial, cultural and tourist centre.

Varna is a vibrant, lively seaside resort, with its own international airport and good main road links between the major cities.

As Bulgaria's third largest city, Varna has been a popular tourist attraction for many years – with a summer season that extends from May to September. Very much an historic city, Varna boasts a wide array of architecturally stunning buildings, some of which are featured in the Photo Gallery of this book.

What sets Varna apart from other tourist destinations within Bulgaria is the fact that although it is predominantly a beach resort, it really is an 'all year round' holiday destination – ideal for city breaks. Varna also offers many cultural attractions, historical buildings, museums and art galleries.

In the peak summer months of July and August it's not uncommon to enjoy over ten hours of sunbathing, across the golden, sandy beaches that stretch across the coastline from the north to the south.

For those of you searching for that perfect place in the sun, Varna offers some spectacular views to the sea and a sea garden that stretches from the city centre out towards the suburbs – providing the most beautiful walks in the park – with calm sea breezes to quicken your steps!

Varna Summer Festival
A thriving metropolis in summer, Varna is host to the *Varna Summer Festival*, a colourful affair of outdoor activities (including classical music, folklore and jazz) that start in June – lining the sea garden and providing a multitude of entertainment for the tourists.

The Varna Summer Festival also includes the Varna jazz festival and an international film festival (usually in August).

Cathedral of the Assumption
Located in the heart of the city centre, the Cathedral of the Assumption is one of the major landmarks in Varna. Constructed in 1886, the gold domed Cathedral of the Assumption contains thrones that have been carved from wood, supported by a pair of winged panthers, carved by craftsmen from Debâr in Macedonia.

Plaza Nezavisimost
Plaza Nezavisimost serves as the main square of Varna, a popular meeting area and has a beautiful fountain that provides a marvellous background for a good variety of restaurants and cafés in this area.

Also situated on Plaza Nezavisimost is the architecturally stunning Opera House – Varna's main cultural institution, with operatic and other musical performances put on all year round.

Starting from early June, the multi-coloured lights are switched on in the fountain – providing a wonderful spectacle, lighting the way for the summer season and the Varna Summer Festival.

Sea Garden

The Sea Garden is the biggest park in Varna, situated right next to the beach. The park area includes the following places of interest:

◆ Seaside Baths

◆ Navy Museum

◆ Museum of Natural History

◆ Aquarium

◆ Astronomical Observatory

◆ Planetarium

◆ Dolphinarium

Look out for the fairground rides and stalls throughout the summer months, which gather around the entrance to the Sea Garden, perfect for children if you are holidaying in Varna during the summer.

Varna by foot

Varna's centre is very easy to explore on foot, with most attractions easily accessible without the need to resort to public transport.

If you are starting in the main square (Plaza Nezavisimost) it takes less than 15 minutes to walk to the beach that's located in the city centre itself. This beach is lined with many restaurants, bars and cafes – which all come alive during the summer months – providing nightclubs and a variety of entertainment.

The beach is clean and sandy, and if you are staying in a hotel or private accommodation in the centre itself, provides the perfect place to entertain children, while the adults can cool down with one of the local beers.

Varna by bus

If you want to head to some of the seaside resorts to the north of Varna it is best to take a local bus – most of the buses stop either in front of or behind the Cathedral which is just across the road from the main square (Plaza Nezavisimost).

Bus tickets are bought from the conductor, with a flat fare of 50 stotinki covering most central city destinations.

Varna by taxi

If you are travelling around Varna by taxi, beware! Some of the taxi drivers are very unscrupulous and you should always insist on them using the meter.

If you feel that the meter is spinning out of control, then I would suggest offering the driver a reasonable amount for the fare. Typically, travelling within the city limits should not cost more than between 2.50-4.50 Leva.

If arriving in Varna from Sofia, then you can typically expect to pay between 2.50 and 3 Leva by taxi to the city centre. If you are charged anything remotely over 5 Leva from the bus station to the city centre, you should refuse and pay the taxi driver a reasonable fare. I was once charged 12 Leva to the city centre, from the bus station – so watch out!

As Paul Greenway points out in his wonderful book on Bulgaria (*Lonely Planet Guide*) – 'the taxi drivers who congregate around the Cathedral are probably the most dishonest bunch of ratbags in Bulgaria'.

Places to visit nearby

As well as being a beach resort in its own right, Varna also provides access to several places of interest including:

◆ St. Constantine

◆ Golden Sands

◆ Albena

◆ Kranevo (quieter seaside village)

◆ Kamchiya (for its nature reserve)

◆ Balchik (for the Queen Marie of Romania's former palace and botanical gardens)

◆ Aladzha (for its rock monastery)

Dracula in Varna!

One interesting discovery that I made whilst researching for this book, is that Varna features in Bram Stokers *Dracula* novel!

'And so, my dear Madam Mina, it is that we have to rest for a time, for our enemy is on the sea, with the fog at his command, on his way to the Danube mouth. To sail a ship takes time, go she never so quick. And when we start to go on land more quick, and we meet him there. Our best hope is to come on him when in the box between sunrise and sunset. For then he can make no struggle, and we may deal with him as we should. There are days for us, in which we can make ready our plan. We know all about where he go. For we have seen the owner of the ship, who have shown us invoices and all papers that can be. The box we seek is to be landed in Varna, and to be given to an agent, one Ristics who will there present his credentials. And so our merchant friend will have done his part. When he ask if there be any wrong, for that so, he can telegraph and have inquiry made at Varna, we say 'no,' for what is to be done is not for police or of the customs. It must be done by us alone and in our own way.' [Bram Stoker, *Dracula* Chapter 24].

Even more interesting is that this research also uncovered a dark secret about the industrial town of Devnya, 30 km west of Varna. Known predominantly for its chemical industry, Devnya had a reputation in the last century as Bulgaria's vampire capital!

In the nineteenth-century, travellers from the Black Sea region revealed that there was widespread belief in vampires among the Bulgarian common folk. In the 1880s, the Czech historian Konstantin Jirecek found a wealth of vampire lore in the isolated rural communities west of Varna.

What Jirecek found were reports of mysterious illnesses among local people being attributed to a visitation by some bloodthirsty evil spirit. Local wise men were paid generously by villagers to drive these demons away. The vampire hunters of Devnya were considered the best in eastern Bulgaria!

VARNA: PROPERTY MARKET

Varna, as a city, has properties to suit all tastes and budgets – with numerous districts within it. *Downtown* – which basically means the city centre area, is amongst the most expensive. If you drive out from the city centre and head east towards the popular Golden Sands resort, you will come to a district called *Briz*, which is an affluent area attracting the rich, successful Bulgarians and an increasing number of foreign investors.

Another popular area for foreign investors is the area known locally as the *Greek Quarter*. This area sits close to the *Sea Garden*, and is therefore only a 5-10 minute walk to the beach. It also represents a good compromise by being close to the sea and also just a few minutes walk to the city centre.

Another area which is said to be good, is the one known for its 'Generals'. Basically, each street is named after a famous General, and this area is quite popular, for example, General Gurko and General Stolipin.

How can I find properties for sale?

To start looking around properties, you can take a walk around the city centre and you will see numerous boards advertising properties for sale by many of the local estate agents. Please don't build your hopes up too much though, as these do tend to be out of date – and it's not uncommon to find that most, if not all, those on display have already been sold!

The best thing to do is to head towards *Maria Luisa Boulevard*, where a good number of the local estate agents are based – and to meet with them to see what they have on offer. Other estate agents are located around this area too. I did hear that there are over 200 estate agent companies competing – so you are really spoilt for choice. If you are travelling to Bulgaria on a viewing trip then its likely that the company has already produced a daily itinerary for you – so in this case, you can sit back and relax – and enjoy the scenery!

In this area you will see a distinct lack of FOR SALE signs. Unlike the UK, Bulgaria has not yet developed its real estate market to the same levels – so sign boards outside houses are quite rare. This makes it difficult to travel around the city yourself looking for properties, simply because you don't have any clear indication of what's for sale! You can, if you like, follow my earlier suggestion and approach restaurant owners, shop keepers or town officials to see if they can point you in the right direction.

What to expect from a new-build

If purchasing a new-build, as indicated earlier, it's likely that it's without any floors in the living room or bedrooms. You can expect to have PVC windows fitted – also within the so-called 'Bulgarian standard'.

When it comes to light fittings and fixtures such as electrical sockets and light switches – these would generally be provided – but do tend to be very simple and you may wish to consider replacing them with a more attractive casing. It is also important to be aware that walls are generally not finished – which usually requires another level of smoothing and a final lick of paint to finish them off. The local builders will describe this as 'smooth and latex', and you can expect to pay, on average about 10 Leva / metre square for this work. In new-builds, the TV cable (combined with internet) is generally left unfinished – leaving you to fix wall sockets etc. You can of course agree with the developer to finish these small items – for an extra fee.

The size of properties is normally advertised in square metres. Do be aware though that the quoted price, particularly for apartments, can sometimes be misleading. This is because they also include any balcony area and outside staircase etc. To be clear on the available space within the living area, ask to see a plan, allowing you to calculate the actual living space yourself. Being situated along the Black Sea Coast, you can find many properties that afford a great view of the sea. If you are buying with the intention to rent, then this is something to consider.

Furnishing your property in Varna

When furnishing your property in Varna, there are numerous shops in the district to choose from. These cater to the majority of your needs, whether you are looking for bathroom specialists, laminate flooring, bathroom tiles, electrical equipment – you will find a good choice both within the city centre and also in some of the large stores such as Technomarket and Metro on the outskirts of the city.

VARNA: GETTING THERE

By air

Travelling from London to Varna, you have a choice of flights with carriers such as Bulgaria Air, Hemus Air, British Airways and Austrian Airways. Whilst Bulgaria Air was flying year round from London Gatwick to Varna, British Airways started year round flights in July 2006.

If you are traveling to Sofia (which you can also do now from London on Wizz Air or Easyjet), you can take a domestic flight to Varna – with Bulgaria Air or Hemus Air.

For more details about flights please refer to Appendix T.

By car

Alternatively, you can consider renting a car from Sofia – with an expected journey time of between 5-6 hours, on relatively good roads for most of the journey if you take the highway.

By coach

There are regular coaches to Varna by a couple of companies from Sofia. 'Biomet' run buses every few hours and provide a comfortable and affordable trip – with the price, at the time of writing, 23 Leva one way (Sofia-Varna). Their buses are very modern, with movies in English and a snack bar on board for hot drinks. Fabulous!

Another company called 'Grup' also operates a service between Sofia and Varna for the same price, and takes just a little longer than 'Biomet' due to a slightly different route (and more stops on the way).

Having personally travelled on both buses I would recommend their services – 'Biomet' provided a great service! The buses are on time, reliable, clean and offer excellent value for money.

One of the other advantages of travelling by bus is that you can enjoy some of the breathtaking scenery on the way – with the undulating hills, small villages and lakes all on display during your 6 hour journey.

19

Living the dream

In this section I am going to introduce you to Chris and Jain Goodall, who moved to Bulgaria in 2004. Attracted by the lower cost of living and better quality of life – almost three years later, they are running a successful monthly magazine called *Quest Bulgaria* and are quite literally *living the dream*.

Having sold their house in South West France, all Chris and Jain needed was their Bulgarian visas (no longer required for EU citizens). Due to delays, they had to rent a house for a few days before they could begin their exciting journey to Bulgaria.

To discover their views and opinions on life in Bulgaria and what may be in store for if you are thinking about a new life in Bulgaria, read on...

What was your plan of action when you were thinking of moving to Bulgaria?

'Our first and most important thing was to make sure we had enough money to live on, so establishing whether the magazine would work was our top priority; talking to Bulgarian businesses, expat Brits in Bulgaria, people wishing to move to Bulgaria, etc. Then came more research about the country, culture, etc. Then finding a place to live. Once we'd established those things, the rest just fell into place.'

Was the move to Bulgaria easy?

'Yes, it was pretty plain sailing really. We decided against moving our furniture ourselves and got in Allied Pickfords from Sofia to do all the packing and removals for us. They were marvellous which meant we could just concentrate in getting in the car and setting off with the dog.

The journey was straight forward all through France, Italy, Greece and then into Bulgaria. Even though we had the dog with us, we easily found hotels willing to take us all in en route. However, we did stay in some rather 'rough' places on the way, so when we arrived in Sofia we were thrilled to espy the Sheraton Hotel and even happier to find they accepted dogs!'

Has life in Bulgaria been good to you?

'Exceptionally good, we wouldn't change it for the world. Mind you, moving out in winter 2004, the Bulgarian temperatures came as quite a shock – coming from south west France where it hardly ever went below zero, we weren't quite prepared for the minus 20 that Sofia threw at us. Even though Chris had been visiting for 20 years it had mainly been in the summer months so it came as a surprise that the +30 degrees he was used had suddenly dropped to –20 degrees!'

What do you like and not like about living in Bulgaria?

'Like – the cost of living, the quality of life overall, our Bulgarian friends, living in Sofia everything is open 24 hours, Bulgarians are very supportive of our business.

Dislike – spitting in the streets, difficulty in getting good beef and good cheeses, street dogs

Living here there are certainly more ups than downs.'

Have you seen many improvements in the country?

'Well, we've been here for nearly three years now and certainly there have been many changes. The most important for anyone who is considering buying a holiday home here is the removal of the need for visas when staying for more than 90 days. The reduction of corporation tax to 10% has been a great move and will help inward investment. The other big recent change has been with the residency permits – this is now a quick and easy process and even the staff at immigration smile when you make your application!'

What are your views on Bulgaria – now that it has joined the EU?

'We're delighted that Bulgaria is in the EU. I think it has made everyone feel much more comfortable with the country and certainly gives a feeling of security. Bulgaria did very well in getting into the EU on time and will now be able to continue the progress on modernisation.

Inevitably with EU funds coming into the country, there will be big progress on badly needed infrastructure. I think the whole country will improve dramatically from now on, so those who have invested here already will find their investment well protected and those yet to invest will be more attracted to the country.'

What prompted you to start the Quest Bulgaria magazine, and are you happy with its growth?

'When Chris and I originally visited Bulgaria together, it was to buy a house. Amazed at the lack of service and decent advice we returned home disappointed. Upon our return we reflected on what was happening in Bulgaria for English speaking people trying to buy property there.

An idea started to form – over ten years ago we had moved to France where we had created and established a magazine to better inform and assist english speaking people considering buying property and even moving there. What was happening in Bulgaria with the lack of correct information, was exactly the same as in France all those years ago. So, we decided not just to buy a house in Bulgaria but to establish an English language magazine again, this time dedicated to helping all those buying and investing in Bulgaria.

We're delighted with its growth - going from just 24 pages in the first edition over two years ago to 80 pages now. It's now the leading specialist English magazine for all things Bulgarian. It's been great and one of the big things our readers like is that everyone working on the magazine lives here and so has first hand experience of the country which we can pass on to them.'

What are your plans for the future in Bulgaria, and what single piece of advice would you give others planning to move to Bulgaria?

'We've been living in Sofia all the time so far, so a country house would be a real treat for us and we've just started looking for a property. For the magazine, we are planning on increasing pagination and print run during the coming year to make the magazine bigger and better for our readers.

Best piece of advice? Well, I would say preparation, realism, accept that things are different here and get at least some language under your belt – that way you'll have freedom and will enjoy Bulgaria, the people and the wonderful culture.'

20

Bulgarian ski resorts

Bulgaria boasts 3 major ski-resorts with millions of euros invested to improve the facilities and infrastructure over the last few years. The ski season typically starts around mid-December and lasts until mid-April, offering up to four months of winter season rental potential.

When buying property in the ski-resorts, you are potentially open to a nine month season (four months in winter and five months in summer). You can possibly make up to twice the returns of similar properties on the Black Sea Coast.

When choosing a rental property on a ski resort, you need to consider how close the development is to the ski-runs – the closer the better; and when deciding between the different resorts consider other factors such as the surrounding areas and other points of attraction. Bankso for example has a beautiful museum town that is attractive all year round and therefore is not dependent purely on the ski season.

Pamporovo does become very quiet out of season but its closeness to Plovdiv – a beautiful historic city that enjoys a real ambience in its old town, about an hour's drive away, means that there are other areas to explore.

Borovets, being just an hour's drive from Sofia, provides the opportunity for tourists to explore the capital city. Sofia is home to many museums, interesting architecture, shopping districts and new, modern shopping malls like the newly built Sofia Mall – a true Western style shopping centre with coffee shops, cafés, branded clothes shops etc.

If you are looking to invest in one of these resorts, here are some essential facts about the three main resorts and some information on prices / rental returns for 2007/2008.

BOROVETS

Borovets is known as the oldest ski resort in Bulgaria and dates back to 1896. It is just one hour away from Sofia (the Bulgarian capital) and stands at 1300m above sea level, in the Rila mountain range. The average temperature during the coldest month January is 4.8°C. With snow coverage from mid December until April, Borovets is located 72km from Sofia, making it the closest resort to Sofia's international airport.

In 2004, an initiative called the *Super Borovets Project* was setup to transform the area into a year-round resort. Expected to run for up to 15 years, the project is estimated to invest over 375 million euros (from both state and private investors) into improving the infrastructure of the region – with football fields, tennis-courts, playgrounds, swimming pools and amusement facilities.

When completed the resort will offer 33 ski pistes with a total length of more than 60 km, quadrupling the capacity for the number of skiers per hour to 10,000.

Rental prices in 2006/2007 averaged €338 per week in the low season, €472 per week in the mid season and €613 per week in the high season. Typical yields would be between 8%–12% based on 70% occupancy during the winter season.

In 2008, property prices in Borovets start from €700 per square metre, reaching up to €1250 per square metre for the top end luxury apartments. A typical studio apartment would cost in the region of €32,000.

BANSKO

Bansko boasts some of the most popular off-plan apartment complexes with property buyers. These apartments typically come with excellent facilities including spa, sauna, fitness rooms, shops and cafes. The most popular apartments tend to be located near to the ski-lifts –attracting the highest rental prices.

Bansko itself is located 160km south of Sofia and is between two to three hours by car. There are two major ski regions in Bansko – Chalin Valog (1100-1600m) and the higher region called Shiligarnika (1700–2500m). Both are situated above the town, on the northern slopes of the Pirin mountain.

One key attraction that Bansko boasts is a beautiful museum town with traditional architecture and a real atmospheric feeling. There are no less than 120 cultural monuments located at the foot of the Pirin mountains. The main landmark of the town being the Holy Trinity Church with its 30m high clocktower.

Having received huge media attention, Bansko is growing in popularity as a destination for winter sports and has had £89 million pounds of investment – with new ski lifts, ticketing system and snow cannons.

On these three developments in Bansko, the annual yields vary between 5–15% – yields obviously being dependent on the success of a particular apartment and its location, facilities, distance to the ski run etc.

To give an example of the kind of rental return you can expect – The Orchard development, from Bulgarian Dreams, is expected to receive the following rental based on occupancy of 70% during the winter season:

Development	Number bedrooms	Low season rental	Mid season rental	High season rental
The Orchard	Studio	€328 per week	€432 per week	€596 per week
The Orchard	1	€449 per week	€596 per week	€771 per week
The Orchard	2	€656 per week	€829 per week	€968 per week

Here, rental yields are expected to vary from 7.44% (1 bedroom), 7.93% (2 bedroom) and 9.52% (studio).

In 2008, property prices in Bansko start from €700 per square metre, reaching up to €1400 per square metre for the top end luxury apartments. A typical studio apartment would cost in the region of €34,000.

PAMPOROVO

Pamporovo, located in the heart of the Rhodophi mountains, is the furthest from Sofia – located 240km away and 85km from Plovdiv. The travel time between Sofia and Pamporovo is approximately three hours.

The resort itself lies at 1620m above sea level, boasting 27 ski runs, with the highest ski run located at 1937m above sea level. There are 4 nursery slopes at the foot of Snejanka peak and along its western slope. It is said that Pamporovo is the sunniest mountain resort in Europe with more than 200 sunny days per year with an average air temperature in winter of –3°C.

The Pamporovo resort is renowned for being well suited for beginners and intermediate skiers. More than 100 highly qualified ski instructors, fluent in several languages, are available to teach both beginners and advanced skiers and an emergency ski patrol service is available 24 hours a day.

Over the last two to three years in particular, there has been significant interest in Pamporovo from developers – and in 2005/2006 has been a strong favourite with property buyers.

An example of rental returns in Pamporovo – Cedar Heights III from Bulgarian Dreams, expects rental returns. based on occupancy of 70% during the winter season, of:

Development	Number bedrooms	Low season rental	Mid season rental	High season rental
Cedar Heights III	Studio	€262 per week	€345 per week	€484 per week
Cedar Heights III	1	€359 per week	€484 per week	€622 per week
Cedar Heights III	2	€524 per week	€663 per week	€929 per week

Expected yields are between 9.35% and 11.97%.

In 2008, property prices in Pamporovo start from €630 per square metre, reaching up to €1250 per square metre for the top end luxury apartments. Generally, prices in Pamporovo are lower than in Bansko. A typical studio apartment would cost in the region of €28,000.

Appendices

APPENDIX A: RENTAL PRICES IN 2008

Let's take a look at a few examples now, to give you an idea of the rental market at the time of writing. *Please remember that this appendix was revised in 2008 and that all prices refer to that year.*

Black Sea Coast

A typical luxury 1 bedroom apartment in a city such as Varna, on the Black Sea Coast, can expect to draw between 300–450 euros a month rental income, on a long term rental.

Looking at a typical 1 bedroom apartment for the short term, you can expect 350 euros a week during the peak season, and 200 euros a week during the off-peak season. The peak season is between June and September, especially for the Black Sea Coastal region.

If you have a villa (for example that sleeps over ten people) then you can expect to rent it out for as much as 800 euros a week in summer, and 350 euros a week in the off-peak season.

A luxury two bedroom apartment near the *Sea Garden* in Varna could expect long term rentals of 850/900 euros a month.

The capital (Sofia)

The average rental price of a luxury apartment in central Sofia in 2008 was between 1000 and 1200 euros per month. This would be on a long term basis (above 12 months) and typically targeted towards foreign businessmen.

In the prestigious *Doctors Garden* district of Sofia you could expect to pay upwards of 1200 euros a month for a luxury two bedroom apartment – peaking at 2000 euros a month.

Unfurnished and furnished houses with nice gardens and professional landscaping on the outskirts of Sofia can fetch rental prices of between 2000 euros and 6000 euros per month. Prices depend on location, size of property, quality, type of furniture etc.

APPENDIX B: LAND PRICES IN 2008

You can expect to pay different prices according to the district that you are buying in. Unfortunately it would not be possible to cover every single district or village in this book. *Obviously, prices are always rising, so this information has to be taken in context, and remember that these prices refer to 2008.*

Looking at investment in plots of land, land prices between 2004 and 2008 increased, on average, by more than 200 per cent. Areas on the Black Sea Coast, such as Golden Sands and Sunny Beach have seen land prices double within a year, reaching in excess of EUR 350/sq m in 2008 for prime plots.

Varna villa zone

In some common villa zones in the Varna district, you can currently pay circa 30–70 euros per square metre. This can be higher as you get closer to the city centre; upwards of 200 euros per square metre.

North of Varna

Driving some 30km of Varna will take you close to the Albena resort – a popular destination for tourists. In this region you will find the villages of Obrochishte and Rogachevo which are both within 4–7km of Albena and provide some fabulous views. Prices here are in the range of 40–55 euros per square metre in Obrochishte and between 30–70 euros per square metre in Rogachevo.

Obrochishte is closer to the Albena resort – being some 4km away and one of the closest villages to Albena itself. It enjoys some amazing panoramic views over the rolling hills and on to neighbouring villages such as Tsurkva ('Church' in English).

Rogachevo has the slight edge over Obrochishte for the views, having a panoramic view over hillsides and a distant sea view looking towards the Albena area.

Near the Albena resort itself you may find yourself paying over 80 euros per square metre for a prime plot of land, but such land is not common to find these days, hence the premium price.

If you drive some 50–60km north of Varna, you will first come to Topola – which enjoys some fabulous sea views and the development of golf courses in the area. Here, it is not uncommon to pay anywhere from 30–80 euros per square metre. With the premium prices of 80 euros per square metre being the plots with the best views on the cliff edge (typically). That is, the *first line* plots.

A little further, you will come to Kavarna, where you can expect to pay upwards of 30 euros per square metre. Kavarna has a larger town area than Topola (which is really a small village). Kavarna benefits from some great coastal plots too, with fabulous sea views.

South of Varna

South of Varna, you will come to areas such as Galata. Galata benefits from being closer to Varna (within ~5 km) and has some great sea views from plots by the coast. Prices here are currently upwards of 50 euros per square metre, on average.

Byala is another popular location for land purchases currently, with average prices between 30–40 euros per square metre. This is also a coastal region that enjoys some fabulous sea views and is proving popular amongst foreign investors.

Taking the road further south to Burgas, you will find that prices here can be as high as 150 euros per square metre for first line plots – especially if you are close to the Sunny Beach resort which has some of the premium properties in the area. In Pomorie, close to Burgas, prices in 2008 were averaging 75 euros per square metre for good, regulated plots.

Sofia

Sofia is a large city, with many districts. To give you an idea of the typical prices of land in Sofia I am going to choose two districts which are proving popular with foreign buyers. These are Dragalevtsi and Vitosha.

In Dragalevtsi a typical regulated plot, suitable for a family mansion, would cost in the region of €90 per square metre. If you are looking for great views of Vitosha mountain, the area of Vitosha has typical regulated land plots for development at €200 per square metre.

In the capital city itself, a regulated plot within 40 metres of the Bulgaria Boulevard would cost in the region of €800 per square metre.

Veliko Turnovo

Veliko Turnovo is a popular tourist location in Bulgaria, steeped in history, stunning scenery and a very scenic old town, where houses appear to be stacked on top of one another.

Being located in the North Central district of Bulgaria, Veliko Turnovo's land prices are significantly lower than those in Sofia and on the coast. You can still buy regulated plots of land in this region for less than €10 per square metre less than a kilometer away from the centre of town. Venturing out by 15 kilometres, you can find land for €3 per square metre.

The most desirable locations in the centre of old town have very few plots available for sale – and these tend to look over the Yantra River, along the famous Gurko Street. If you are lucky enough to find a plot available for sale here, you are looking at between €200–€300 per square metre. You do have to take into account that plots are typically very small – with plots of 80–100 square metres not uncommon.

Bansko

Bansko has been a very popular location for property developers over the last two to three years in particular. Due to the millions of euros being invested in this premium ski resort, land prices have been appreciating well.

Currently, looking at regulated plots within 5–7 kilometres of Bansko can cost in the region of €25–€50 per square metre. Further out, as you move beyond 10 kilometres away, you can purchase land plots for €18–€19 per square metre. Approximately 5 kilometres away from Bansko in the town of Razlog, typical plots are selling for €35 per square metre in 2008.

Plovdiv

Plovdiv is the second largest town in Bulgaria, and like Veliko Turnovo, benefits from a charming old town that creates a real atmosphere of times gone by. Located in the South Central region of Bulgaria, Plovdiv is both an architectural and historical reserve.

With many villages in the region, prices typically vary between €10–€20 per square metre within villages located in a radius of 10 kilometres from Plovdiv. Venturing out further, you can buy plots of land for as low as €4 per square metre some 25 kilometres away.

If you fancy a plot in the old part of town, you could be looking at €650 per square metre for a plot on which you can build your 4-storey mansion – reaching up to €1000 per square metre at the high end.

APPENDIX C: AVERAGE NEW APARTMENT PRICES IN BULGARIA IN 2008

The prices for property will vary according to a number of factors – typically governed by:

◆ Location

◆ Amenities

◆ Build quality

◆ Type of building

◆ Amount of land that comes with the property

◆ Time (property prices are not static!)

The table below provides an illustration of how much you would typically pay per square metre based on the prices of **apartments** in the major cities of Bulgaria:

City	Average price (per m^2) in 2008
Sofia	925 EUR
Plovdiv	600 EUR
Varna	900 EUR
Burgas	750 EUR
Veliko Turnovo	500 EUR
Bansko	900 EUR
Pamporovo	1000 EUR

If you compare these prices to similar properties in Central and Eastern Europe, then you would find prices in excess of 2,000 euros per square metre.

The following table from the National Statistical Institute of Bulgaria (NSI) presents the price in leva per square metre for several districts across Bulgaria.

District centres	Average prices – Levs/sq.m	
	2006	**2007**
1 Blagoevgrad	797.9	1 038.67
2 Burgas	1 227.0	1 442.08
3 Varna	1 316.0	1 762.63
4 Veliko Tarnovo	811.1	968.92
5 Vidin	587.6	802.28
6 Vratsa	637.8	825.13
7 Gabrovo	620.9	771.92
8 Kardzhali	628.8	727.88
9 Kyustendil	459.2	601.58
10 Lovech	540	646.13
11 Montana	641.3	778.67
12 Pazardzhik	588.4	720.63
13 Pernik	656	918.21
14 Pleven	769.5	1 004.46
15 Plovdiv	940.3	1 143.17
16 Razgrad	558.2	744.17
17 Ruse	895.7	1 262.00
18 Silistra	461.7	640.29
19 Sliven	670.2	822.17
20 Smolyan	712.2	839.52
21 Sofia cap.	1 341.8	1 813.17
22 Sofia	411.7	488.14
23 Stara Zagora	914.6	1 144.75
24 Dobrich	589.4	743.75
25 Targovishte	586	845.46
26 Haskovo	740.6	922.71
27 Shumen	676	819.46
28 Yambol	591.2	683.47

Source: National Statistical Institute, Bulgaria 2008

In Sofia, between 2003 and 2008, some of the properties have more than tripled in price.

From 2003 to 2008 real estate prices, on average, have increased by over 100 per cent. For those early birds who purchased property on the Black Sea Coast in 2002/2003 (for example), they could see their investments more than double by 2008/2009.

Analysts have predicted a steadier growth in real estate prices from 2008, with many quoting average growth of 10–15% annually. Those investors looking to achieve higher rates of growth need to study the Bulgarian market more closely to determine where the next growth areas are likely to be.

Looking at the current prices in central Bulgaria – in districts like Veliko Turnovo and Elena – various projects, funded by British investors, suggest room for growth in these regions and an upbeat optimism about the potential of rural hamlets.

Following Bulgaria's accession to the EU in January 2007, more foreign investment is coming into the country – and its capital city, Sofia, is going to see ongoing development of its infrastructure, facilities and real estate market. Just driving through Sofia in 2008, you cannot help but notice a hive of activity with the construction of modern apartment complexes, particularly along the Bulgaria Boulevard – a large road that leads into the city's centre.

APPENDIX D: MOST POPULAR PLACES TO BUY PROPERTY

There is no doubt that the Black Sea Coast is attracting many foreign investors. It is also attracting a growing number of Europeans (particularly) who are either buying or building their own villas for retirement.

Inland, foreign buyers are snapping up country properties from as little as 7,500 euros for a small house with land (perhaps between 600–1,000 square metres).

Historic centres, further inland, such as Veliko Turnovo are also proving popular places to buy. Veliko Turnovo is approximately 3 hours by car from Sofia, and acts as a mid-way point between Sofia and Varna. In fact, if you take a bus to Varna, from Sofia, the chances are that it will stop in Veliko Turnovo on the way.

The following locations were among the top favourites to buy property over the past few years:

◆ Sofia

◆ Sunny Beach

◆ Bansko

◆ Pamporovo

◆ Varna

◆ Burgas

◆ Veliko Turnovo

APPENDIX E: REAL ESTATE MARKET INDEX

The Real Estate Market Index (REMI) was established in September 2002 for investment activities on the Bulgarian market. Bulgaria is the first country in Central and Eastern Europe which has established a national Property Index.

The REMI displays data from the 157 members of the National Real Property Association (NRPA) in Bulgaria, which hold 80 per cent of the Bulgarian Property Market.

Bulgarian and foreign property investors, financial institutions, administration, consultants in the area of Real Estates etc., can benefit from the information that Bulgarian Property Index provides.

As the graph below shows, the real estate market in Bulgaria remains on an upward trend – and started to grow more significantly from the start of June / July 2003.

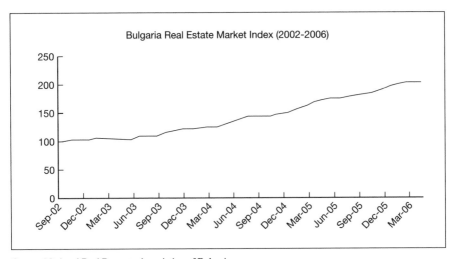

Source: National Real Property Association of Bulgaria

APPENDIX F: PROPERTY GUIDE FROM €3000 TO €1,000,000

In 2008, the range of residential property available in Bulgaria starts from as low as €3000 and at the extreme end of the scale, over €1,000,000. In this section, I will give you an idea of what you can get for your hard earned cash, based on your budget.

€3000 – for just under €3000 you can buy a 2-storey rural property in need of major renovation near Lovech (North Central Bulgaria).

€5000 – will get you a small rural house (in need of renovation) near Pleven (North Central Bulgaria) with over 2000m² of garden!

€10,000 – will get you a two bedroom house, requiring renovation and modernization, 15km away from Vidin (North West Bulgaria), on a plot of just over 1000m².

€15,000 – is going to get you a three bedroom house in Yambol (South East Bulgaria), in a rural setting, requiring modernization, with a garden of over 2000 m²

€20,000 – will get you a house, barn and garden just 25km away from Veliko Turnovo. It would require painting, modernatisation to bring it up to Western standards.

€25,000 – is enough to buy a new studio apartment in Sunny Beach – a popular summer resort on the South East coast of Bulgaria.

€30,000 – will get you a studio apartment on a complex in Pamporovo – one of the popular ski resorts in Bulgaria.

€35,000 – can even get you a renovated 4 bedroom house in Haskovo (South Central Bulgaria), complete with 200 m² of living space and a view over a pine-wood.

€40,000 – will get you a first line sea view studio apartment in Sozopol (new part of town).

€45,000 – can provide you with a renovated 2 bedroom house some 28km away from Veliko Turnovo with a large garden.

€50,000 – will get you a brand new 1 bedroom apartment in the Dragalevtsi district of Sofia, just 7km away from the Sofia international airport. This is a popular area, with many mansions and diplomatic family residences.

€55,000 – can get you a 2 bedroom family house in Vidin (North West Bulgaria), near the Danube river – complete with landscaped gardens.

€60,000 – will buy you a 2 bedroom apartment in Bansko – one of the most prestigious ski resorts in Bulgaria.

€65,000 – will buy you a 4 bedroom house 15km away from Borovets, with some minor renovation on the lower floor. Borovets is another popular ski resort location in Bulgaria.

€70,000 – will get you a 4 bedroom refurbished house 42km away from Plovdiv, in a small town.

€75,000 – will get you a 5 bedroom house in need of modernisation in the region of Elhovo (South East Bulgaria).

€80,000 – is ideal for those families looking for a 2 bedroom apartment in Bansko, with just a 12 minute walk to the Gondola!

€85,000 – will get you a 1 bedroom luxury apartment in the very popular Lozenets district of Sofia – a desirable rental location, offering good rental potential.

€90,000 – will get you a 4 bedroom house, 23km away from Bansko and with over 250m^2 of living space!

€95,000 – will get you a 5 bedroom, 2 storey home near Elhovo, with a garden of 700m^2, with a 20 minute drive to the border with Turkey.

€100,000 – will get you a spacious 2 bedroom apartment in the Lozenets district of Sofia, very close to the South Park OR you could buy a 4 bedroom villa 12km away from Elena (North Central Bulgaria).

€125,000 – will get you a luxury renovated 2 bedroom house near Veliko Turnovo.

€150,000 – will let you splash out on a 6 bedroom house in Borovets, looking over a pine forest, with 450m^2 of living space!

€175,000 – will get you a luxury 2 bedroom villa with fabulous views in the town of Primorsko, 15km away from the seaside town of Tsarevo.

€200,000 – will get you a large 2-storey hotel 32km away from Veliko Turnovo, with over 450m^2 of living space.

€250,000 – will get you a 150 year old stone house with 6 bedrooms and 5 bathrooms just 10km away from Pamporovo (the popular ski resort).

€300,000 – will get you a 3 bedroom new house in the Gorna Banya district of Sofia.

€350,000 – will buy you a luxury 4/5 bedroom mansion with a sea view near the Albena beach resort in the Varna region – a popular summertime destination.

€400,000 – is the asking price for 2 storey, 3 bedroom luxury apartments in the Lozenets district of Sofia.

€500,000 – will get you a brand new 3 bedroom luxury house in the Boyana district of Sofia, popular with diplomats.

€1,000,000 – so just what can you get for 1 million euros? You can buy a top-end ultra luxury, furnished 3 bedroom apartment, with an unobstructed sea view in the sea garden of Varna, OR a 4 bedroom, 3 bathroom exclusive property with fabulous views over Sofia city, in the Boyana district of Sofia.

APPENDIX G: TRANSFERRING MONEY ON XETRADE, IN TEN STEPS

1. To transfer money on XETrade, first login to the website on www.xetrade.com (assuming that you have already set up an account).

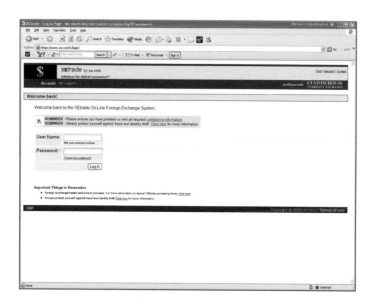

2. Select the **Basic Trade** option to **buy** currency at the current exchange rate.

3. Enter the amount of euros that you want to buy – specifying the currency to buy as **euros** (recommended for Bulgaria) and the currency to sell as **GBP** (assuming you are based in the UK, for example). Here, we are buying 1,000 euros (which may be for the initial deposit on a plot of land, for example).

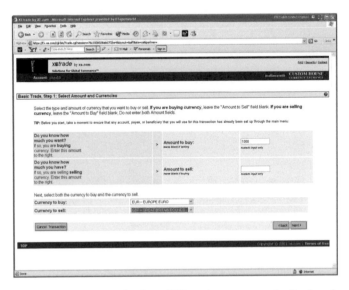

4. Specify the payment method as **Wire** (recommended), for the method that the payment will be sent to your Bulgarian bank and also the method that you will use to transfer the money to XETrade:

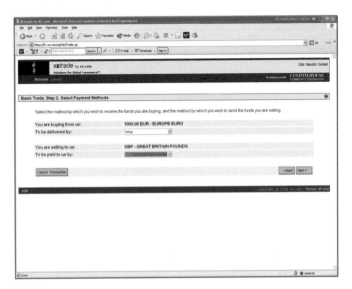

5. Select where you are going to transfer the money to (i.e. your Bulgarian bank account which you set up earlier) and provide a reference so that you can identify the transaction:

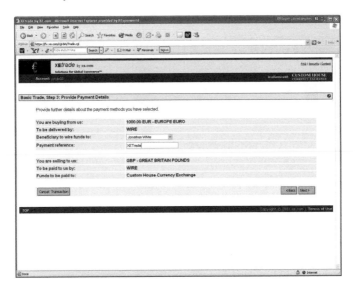

6. Press the **Confirm Trade!** button to confirm the trade – assuming you are happy with the exchange rate (shown here as 1.46680022):

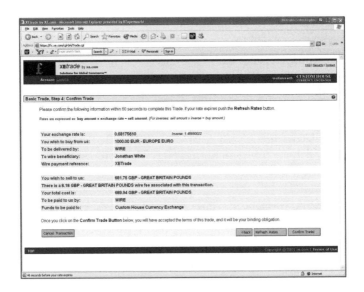

Note: You can see exactly how much you are being charged for the wire transfer to your Bulgarian bank account – here, it is £8.18.

7. You will then receive confirmation by email that your trade has been entered and a screen will be displayed also providing you with a reference for the transaction.

8. You must then wait for an email that informs you that your trade is PROCESSING and that you must now transfer what you owe XETrade.

This email would typically look like this:

'This message is to notify you that we have begun processing the Basic Trade that you recently booked through XE.com's XEtrade online foreign exchange system.

Status	: **PROCESSING**
Trade Type	: Basic Trade
Deal Number	: W00012345A
Booked at	: August 21, 04 at 13:47:36 AM PST (GMT-8)
You are Buying	: 1000.00 EUR
You are Selling	: 689.94 GBP
Payment Method	: Wire Transfer

You selected to pay for this order by Wire Transfer. Please ensure that you initiate a Wire Transfer with your banking institution as soon as possible to cover the full settlement amount of this trade: 689.94 GBP.

Afterwards, please send us the date and time that you initiated this Wire Transfer in a reply to this e-mail message. This will assist us in processing your transaction.'

9. You can pay XETrade by using your UK internet bank account – transferring the amount in GBP (£689.94 in this example) identified by 'Your Total Cost' (step 6 above) to the bank account that XETrade have setup. XETrade's bank account is identified by the account

Custom House Currency Exchange. You are provided with the details of this account when you confirm your transaction through the XETrade system.

By using your internet bank account to transfer the money (GBP) to XETrade, you save yourself money, because there would be no cost associated with the transfer to XETrade this way. If you were to send the money by CHAPS instead, it would typically cost you £23 for the transfer (by comparison).

10. When your trade has been completed, an email will be sent by XETrade confirming that the transfer has been completed.

This email would typically look like this:

'This message is to notify you that we have begun processing the Basic Trade that you recently booked through XE.com's XEtrade online foreign exchange system.

Status	: **COMPLETED**
Trade Type	: Basic Trade
Deal Number	: W00012345A
Value Date	: August 21, 04 at 13:47:36 AM PST (GMT-8)
You Bougt	: 1,000.00 EUR
You Sold	: 689.94 GBP
Delivery Method	: Wire Transfer
Wire Sent	: August 24, 2004

The Wire Transfer for the funds you purchased was wired to your selected Wire Beneficiary on the date specified above.

If the funds are not received within Five (5) business days of that date, please contact us in a reply to this message so that we can initiate a trace on the funds.'

♦ TOP TIP ♦

You should set up a Bulgarian bank account that has internet access. After receiving the above email confirmation, you can check your Bulgarian bank account on the internet over the next couple of days to check when the funds have been transferred.

This means that you can achieve the whole transfer process electronically, without involving anyone else – all in the comfort of your own home!

APPENDIX H: USEFUL WEBSITES

Tourism, hotels, private apartment links
http://www.varnarentals.com
http://www.villa-vacation.com
http://varna.info.bg/english/default.htm
http://www.bulgaria.com/varna/
http://www.beachbulgaria.com/varna/index.shtml
http://www.holiday-rentals.co.uk
http://www.vacationvillas.net
http://www.netaway.co.uk/villas-search.php
http://www.varnahotels.com
http://www.bulgaria-hotels.com/

Satellite and Cable TV links
http://www.lyngsat.com/
http://www.astra2d.co.uk/
http://www.itvpartner.com
http://www.m-sat.bg

Internet Service Providers
http://www.netbg.com/
http://www.internet-bg.net/e/index0.htm
http://www.btc.bg/en
http://www.einet.bg/en/index.html
http://www.varna.net/Eng/index.html
http://www.spnet.net
http://www.bulgaria.com/links/internet.html
http://www.digsys.bg/company_eng.html
http://www.bulinfo.net/index_en.html

Car hire
http://www.visitbulgaria.net/rentacar/
http://www.e-sixt.com/main?/extern/carhire/classic/Bulgaria
http://www.motoroads.com
http://www.bogicars.com

Internet forums on Bulgaria and Bulgarian property
http://www.mybulgaria.info
http://www.britsinbulgaria.org/forum
http://www.propertydragon.com/forum

Magazines
http://www.questbg.com
http://www.vagabond-bg.com

News sites
http://www.bulgariadaily.com/
http://www.novinite.com
http://www.sofiaecho.com/
http://www.capital.bg/
http://www.pari.bg/
http://www.onlinebg.com/

Address finder for Bulgarian addresses, cities and resorts etc.
http://www.bgmaps.com
http://www.guide-bulgaria.com

Investment
http://investbg.government.bg

Companies based in Bulgaria that deal with property

Inspired Ideas	http://www.inspiredideasltd.com
Bulgarian Properties	http://www.BulgarianProperties.com/
Foros	http://www.forosbg.com/
Kirov	http://www.kirov.bg/
Address	http://www.address.bg/
Viviun	http://www.viviun.com/Real_Estate/Bulgaria/
Trust	http://www.trust-estates.com/
DAO Real	http://www.daoreal.com/
Adis	http://www.adis.bg/
Atrium	http://www.atriumbg.com/
BG Properties	http://www.bg-properties.com/
Imoti BG	http://www.imotibg.com/
Stara Planina	http://www.stara-planina.com
Key Century Homes	http://www.keycenturyhomes.com

UK-based companies that deal with property in Bulgaria

Global Spaces	http://www.globalspaces.co.uk
EasyBG	http://www.easybg.com/
Bulgarian Dreams	http://www.bulgariandreams.com/
Zoldi BG Property	http://www.zoldibg.com/
A Bulgarian Dream	http://www.getonit.co.uk/bulgarianproperty/
Avatar International	http://www.avatar-bulgaria.com/
Balkan Villas	http://www.balkanskichalet.com/
Anglo-Bulgarian Properties	http://www.anglobulgarian.borsabg.com/
Bulgarian Apartments and Adventures	http://www.bg-aa.com/
Bulgaria Revealed	http://www.bulgariarevealed.com/
Barrasford & Bird	http://www.barrasfordandbird.co.uk/
Knight International	http://www.bulgaria-property.com/

Airlines

Bulgaria Air	http://www.air.bg/en/
British Airways	http://www.britishairways.com/
Hemus Air	http://www.hemusair.bg/

Flights

Wefly.co.uk	http://www.wefly.co.uk
Bargainholidays.com	http://www.bargainholidays.com
Thomson Flights	http:// www.thomsonfly.com
Co-op Travel Shop	http://www.cooptravelshop.co.uk
Budget Travel	http://www.budgettravel.ie
Direct Holidays	http://www.directholidays.ie
Cheap Flights	http://www.cheapflights.co.uk
Just the Flight	http://www.justtheflight.co.uk
Charter Flights	http://www.charterflights.co.uk
Balkan Holidays	http://www.balkanholidays.co.uk
First Choice	http://www.firstchoice.co.uk
XL Airways	http://ie.xl.com
Sunway	http://www.sunwayholidays.ie
Easyjet	http://www.easyjet.com

Banks

CB Allianz Bulgaria	http://bank.allianz.bg
Bulbank	http://www.bulbank.bg
First Investment Bank	http://www.fibank.bg
Postbank	http://www.postbank.bg
ING Bank	http://www.ing.bg

Property search sites (for property buyers)

PropertyDragon	http://www.propertydragon.com
Primelocation	http://www.primelocation.com
FindaProperty	http://www.findaproperty.com
Rightmove	http://www.rightmove.co.uk
PropertyFinder	http://www.propertyfinder.com

Sites to advertise property (for property sellers)

PropertyDragon	http://www.propertydragon.com
Number One 4 Property	http://numberone4property.co.uk
The Movechannel.com	http://www.themovechannel.com
The Little House Company	http://www.thelittlehousecompany.co.uk
HouseWeb	http://www.houseweb.com

Mortgages for property in Bulgaria

BulgarianHomeLoans	http://www.bulgarianhomeloans.com
Conti Financial Services	http://www.mortgageoverseas.com
Moneysprite	http://www.moneysprite.com

Stock Photography sites featuring Bulgaria

FotoFriction	http://www.fotofriction.com
BulgariaPhotos	http://www.bulgariaphotos.net
StockaPhoto	http://www.stockaphoto.com
iStockPhoto	http://www.istockphoto.com
Inmagine	http://www.inmagine.com

Furniture shops / online stores

Furniture Shop Varna	http://www.furniture-shop-varna.com
Bulgarian Furniture Online	http://bgfurnitureonline.com
Bulgaria Furniture	http://www.bulgariafurniture.com
Como	http://www.como.bg

APPENDIX I: USEFUL CONTACT INFORMATION

Insurance companies

QBE International Insurance Limited
Sofia branch, 8 Iskar Street,
1000, Sofia,
Bulgaria.

tel:	+359 (0)2 930 1919
fax:	+359 (0)2 930 1920
website:	http://www.qbe-sofia.bg

Allianz Bulgaria Holding AD
59, Dondukov Blvd.,
1504, Sofia,
Bulgaria

tel:	+ 359 (0)2 988 01 06
	+ 359 (0)2 846 83 78
fax:	+ 359 (0)2 980 52 01
website:	http://www.allianz.bg

Currency Exchange companies

Xchange Business Foreign Currency Brokers
Old Fishmarket Close
The Royal Mile
Edinburgh
EH1 1RW
Scotland, UK.

tel:	0800 953 1384 (freephone within the UK)
tel:	+44 131 622 0087 (from outside the UK)
website:	http://www.foreign-currency-exchange.co.uk/

Moneycorp
2 Sloane Street
Knightsbridge
London
SW1X 9LA

tel: +44 (0)20 7808 0500
website: http://www.moneycorp.co.uk/pages/home.html

XE.com
330 Bay Street
Suite 1109
Toronto
MSH 2S8
Canada

tel: +1 416 214-5606
website: http://www.xe.com/fx/

British Bulgarian Chamber of Commerce

British Bulgarian Chamber of Commerce – UK
PO Box 123
Bromley
BR1 4ZX
United Kingdom

tel: +44 (0)20 8464 5007
fax: +44 (0)20 8464 5007
e-mail: info@bbcc.bg
website: http://www.bbcc.bg

British Bulgarian Chamber of Commerce – Sofia
8 Charles Darwin Str.
1113 Sofia
Bulgaria

tel: +359 2 971 4756
fax: +359 2 738 331
e-mail: info@bbcc.bg

Recommended law firm
'Dobreva & Boneva'
Maria Boneva Attorney at Law – Senior Partner
Maria Dobreva Attorney at Law – Senior Partner
9, Dragoman Str
Floor 3
Varna
BG 9000, Bulgaria

tel/fax: +359 52 605006
e-mail: lawfirm@evko.com

Recommended accountancy
SB Assets Management Ltd
Svetlan Bonev CA
9, Dragoman Str
Floor 3
Varna
BG 9000, Bulgaria

tel/fax: +359 52 699789
e-mail: sbonev@sbam.co.uk

Tourist related information
MINISTRY OF ECONOMY
Deputy Minister of Tourism
4 Lege Str.
1000 Sofia

tel: +359 2 980 7483
fax: +359 2 981 2515
e-mail: tourism@mi.government.bg

BULGARIAN CHAMBER OF TOURISM (BCT)
8, Sveta Sofia Str.
1040 Sofia

tel: +359 2 987 4059
fax: +359 2 986 5133

BULGARIAN ASSOCIATION FOR RURAL AND ECOLOGICAL TOURISM (BARET)
BAN, bl. 3, room 320
Akademik Angel Bonchev Str.
1113 Sofia

tel:	+359 2 979 3363
tel/Fax:	+359 2 971 3485
e-mail:	baret@aster.net

BULGARIAN ASSOCIATION OF TOURIST AGENCIES (BATA)
4 Triaditsa Str., floor 5
1000 Sofia

tel:	+359 2 981 7790
fax:	+359 2 981 4580
e-mail:	bata@mail.orbitel.bg

Recommended reading

Bulgaria: Lonely Planet, 1st Edition, 2002 (ISBN 1–86450–148–0)
Bulgaria Euro Country Map, Geocenter, 2004 (ISBN 3–575–03106–1)

APPENDIX J: PRACTICAL TIPS – BEFORE YOU GO TO BULGARIA

	Consideration	Tip
1	Satisfy yourself that you have a basic grounding about Bulgaria	Research the various books, magazines and internet sites on Bulgaria.
2	Determine your budget	Assess what you can buy with your allocated budget.
3	Fully research the process of buying a home	Your Bulgarian solicitor should be your best friend!
4	If you are buying for investment, are you looking for a rental income or capital growth?	Contact other investors via internet forums or property seminars to see what they are getting for rental and/or capital growth.
5	Visit the country first before you buy	You wouldn't generally buy a car without taking a test drive first, so why should buying a home be any different! So, book a viewing trip.
6	What kind of property do you want to buy?	Research the issues surrounding the purchase of a house or apartment – e.g. setting up a company is required for property with land.
7	Arrange a viewing trip with either a UK or Bulgarian agency	This will be invaluable in your search for a property and is certainly more advisable than a blind purchase over the internet.
8	Determine the type of location you want for your property and research the local geography.	Use travel guides and advice from agencies to determine the types of locations that are right for you. Take the time to visit several locations.
9	Set out the criteria for your viewing trip and send it to the company that you are using.	For a successful viewing trip, make a list of what you are looking for and ensure you communicate this with the agency that you use.
10	When planning your viewing trip, do take into account the distances between the regions you are looking at.	Research the distances between different locations. You would be hard pushed to view several properties in both Varna and Burgas all in one day (unless you were prepared to go into the late evening!)
11	Bulgarian properties generally advertise land and room sizes in square metres.	Multiply the number of square metres by 10.76 to get square feet if you haven't gone metric yet!
12	Please don't set your heart on just one or two properties that you find on the internet and fly out to Bulgaria on a whim.	Research more about Bulgaria – expect to view many properties before you find the one for you – and give it time!

APPENDIX K: PRACTICAL TIPS – BUYING A PROPERTY

	Consideration	Tip
1	Get legal advice	Preferably employing the services of a local Bulgarian solicitor.
2	Get tax advice	Preferably employing the services of a local Bulgarian accountant.
3	Use agencies and estate agents to assist you in finding your property.	Unless you are fluent in Bulgarian or are more adventurous than most, I would recommend you use the services of a professional agency.
4	Ensure that the ownership of the property is legal.	Your Bulgarian solicitor will check the documents, but do try to get an independent solicitor – not the solicitor that the agency appoints.
5	Think about any potential renovation costs	If you are buying an older property this is particularly important.
6	Who will look after your property when you are away?	Look into hiring the services of a property management company. Some of the professional agencies and estate agents provide this service too.
7	Pay the deposit at the preliminary contract signing stage, not before. The deposit is normally 10%.	Don't be persuaded to part with the deposit before you have signed the preliminary contract. You should only agree to a maximum 10% deposit.
8	If you do not plan to live in the property yourself, consider the security of the property.	You can install a security system that is tied to a company that can respond within minutes, and also arrange for your neighbours to look after your property.
9	Check that the property has the utilities that the estate agent claims.	Ask your solicitor to check that the property has the electricity, water and telephone access (as applicable).
10	If buying a new property, ensure that it has its certificate for 'permission to use'.	The certificate for 'permission to use, is issued by the local authorities when the property is deemed 'liveable'.
11	If using an agency, ask them to be upfront about ALL the costs of purchasing a property.	If you are paying a fixed price to an agency, you may find that there are still some additional costs – so it pays to request ALL costs to be outlined.
12	Avoid buying property directly from the internet.	Unless you visit the properties in person, you do not really know what problems may be waiting for you.

	Consideration	**Tip**
13	Ask for recommendations of good estate agents and agencies.	Join the internet forums and try to establish which agents are more reliable.
14	Shop around for the best price when setting up a Bulgarian company.	You will be quoted prices ranging from 600 euros to over 1,200 euros. Shop around for agencies that provide the most competitive fee.
15	Be prepared to find more than one property to avoid disappointment.	Due to the fast pace with which properties are being snapped up, it's best to find more than one property that you are prepared to make an offer on.
16	Ask your solicitor to check that the property is not in a landslide area (or 'red zone').	This is even more important when buying in some of the coastal areas on the Black Sea Coast – more so on the North Black Sea Coast.
17	Arrange to get your preliminary contract and notary deed translated into English.	This is important and should be done at the same time that the Bulgarian version is produced so that you know what you are signing.
18	If you can, try to be present for the signing of the notary deed.	This is the final stage, upon which you will take ownership of your property. You are best advised to be present yourself, or give your spouse/partner power of attorney to do it on your behalf.
19	Remember to take your passports with you when you go to sign either the preliminary contract or notary deed.	You will have to visit the notary public who will authorise the contracts and as part of this process he/she will need to verify the identity of the buyer(s) and seller(s).
20	Bring some spare cash to pay the notary public for their service.	There are fees to pay the notary public for their service.
21	If you have formed a company, check your paperwork.	After you have successfully registered a company, you should be provided with (a) company registration papers (in Bulgarian), (b) a company stamp and (c) a company tax registration card (slightly larger than a credit card).
22	Negotiate the estate agent commissions.	Estate agents typically expect 3% commission in Bulgaria, unless they are particularly greedy. There is nothing to lose in negotiating this rate.
23	Set out the criteria for your viewing trip and send it to the company that you are using.	For a successful viewing trip, make a list of what you are looking for and ensure you communicate this with the agency that you use.

	Consideration	Tip
24	Be prepared for differences in attitudes and behaviour during the sale.	It is not uncommon, as highlighted in this book, for sellers to force you to pull out of the deal for a multitude of reasons. Be prepared for this, and always have other options lined up.
25	If possible (and time permits) visit as many estate agents as you can.	It helps to understand how estate agents work, and to compare the quality, services, prices and professionalism of these agencies.
26	Ask the estate agents up front about their fees for viewing properties or land.	Some agents charge a fee based on mileage. Others don't charge at all. Always ask the agent to be clear about any charges due, **before** you look at the properties/land.
27	Older houses (e.g. on two levels) may have an external staircase connecting the upper and lower floors.	Be prepared for this! It will affect the renovation costs and may even lead to you demolishing the existing property.
28	The toilet may be in the garden on older properties.	Again – be prepared! Factor this into the renovation costs.
29	Whatever you read in magazines or see on television, do not expect to buy a property that is ready to move into (by western standards) for 7000 euros or even close to that!	Follow my advice and set out your criteria as detailed in Chapter 4 – and use one of the real estate agents to advise you whether your expectations are realistic.
30	If at first you don't succeed, try, try again!	You may find that your first attempt at purchasing a property fails. If this is the case, try not to be too disheartened and try again.

APPENDIX L: PRACTICAL TIPS – MANAGING YOUR FINANCES

	Consideration	Tip
1	Determine how you are going to transfer money to Bulgaria.	Use one of the currency exchange companies or websites to transfer euros to a bank account in Bulgaria.
2	Open a local bank account in euros.	The majority of properties in Bulgaria are advertised in euros, even though the local currency is the Leva.
3	Shop around for a bank that provides a good internet banking service.	This is important if you need to monitor your accounts from your home country.
4	Use an internet-based system to transfer money to Bulgaria.	This is very convenient and means that you can perform the transactions in the comfort of your own home (assuming you have internet access).
5	Ensure that you allow up to 10% for the initial deposit.	10% is the normal amount to pay for the initial payment (at the time of signing the preliminary contract).
6	Allow sufficient funds to cover the legal costs and any agency fees.	Legal costs include the cost of solicitor fees, notary public fees – whilst agency fees include commissions, transport costs for viewing property etc.
7	If you are not based in a country whose currency is not based on euros then do watch for market fluctuations in the currency exchange as this will affect your purchase.	Currency exchange fluctuations can affect the price you pay for the property. If possible, buy euros when the rate is good, or take a forward option to retain the current rate for a certain number of days (to avoid fluctuations).
8	Take into account the government related taxes for any property or land that you buy.	Government taxes can equate to approximately 3.5%.
9	If you are viewing properties with a local estate agent you may have to pay towards the cost of petrol for any viewings that you make.	It would be advisable to take some cash, in Leva, to cover the petrol costs. A typical day may cost you between 20 and 70 Leva depending on which company you use.
10	When it comes to the final payment, consider the most convenient means of payment for **you**.	You may be requested to pay the final payment in cash. You should try to insist on a bank transfer, as this is safer and potentially cheaper for you. This is because some banks in Bulgaria charge you for withdrawing money from your bank account.

APPENDIX M: PRACTICAL TIPS – RENTING OUT YOUR PROPERTY

	Consideration	Tip
1	Consider how easy it is to rent in the area you are looking at.	Look at the property rental web sites on the internet to gauge the rental prices and availability of properties for rent in this area.
2	If you want to rent out your property, assess the market prices.	You can search property rental websites for property in Bulgaria or ask local estate agents for indicative prices of rental properties.
3	Find a property management company to manage your property.	A number of estate agents provide property management services and over time more independent companies will start up to provide these services. Meet with some estate agents and compare their prices and services to establish who provides the best value for money. Ask for references.
4	Market your property on a website, for global advertising.	There are a number of internet sites that provide advertising for properties in different countries – specifically for those looking for private holiday villas or apartments. Register with such sites to increase your exposure.
5	Ensure that you cater for any damage to your property.	For short-term rentals consider charging a damage deposit.
6	Look at installing either cable TV or satellite.	Cable TV has a monthly charge, where as satellite offers a free to air option, meaning that you only have to pay the initial installation / equipment fees. Installing satellite TV may work out cheaper in the long run.
7	Consider how tenants will get to your property (short-term rental)	Arrange for pickup from the airport, for example.
8	Consider police registration (short-term rental)	Organise someone to assist with the police registration process.
9	How will your tenants feel when they arrive (short-term rental)?	Provide tea/coffee making faciltities, powdered milk, sugar etc.
10	For medium to long-term rentals, consider who will pay the utility bills.	It is common to ask the tenants to pay the utility bills in addition to the rent.

APPENDIX N: SAMPLE PRELIMINARY CONTRACT

PRELIMINARY CONTRACT
FOR THE SALE TRADE OF A REAL ESTATE

Today 06.02.2004, in Varna, on the grounds of Art. 19 from the Law concerning the Obligations and Contracts, was concluded the present Contract between:

1. Nick Dobranov, Personal No. 1234567890 – Varna

2. Emil Dobranov, Personal No. 2345678901 – Varna

herein referred to as the **SELLERS** on the one hand and:

1. John Smith, date of birth 08.07.1968, passport number No. 345678901, issued 23.12.1996

2. Maria Jane, date of birth 15.03.1977, passport number No. 456789012, issued 07.02.1997

herein referred to as the **BUYERS** on the other hand for the following:

I.   SUBJECT OF THE CONTRACT

1.1. The SELLER sells to the BUYER the following real estate, namely: apartment, located in the town of Varna, 14 'General Tsankov', garret living floor and consisting – for apartment '1': antre, bathroom and WC, kitchen boxing, living room, two bedrooms and three balconies with constructed area of 77.10 sq. m. for apartment '2': antre, bathroom and WC, kitchen boxing, living room, bedroom with constructing area of 50.10 sq. m as well as share due from the common parts of the building and as well as corresponding ideal parts from the plot with 461 sq. m from the total area of the property, for the amount of 60,000 EUR.

The present estate is described according to an Ownership document No. 122, volume IX, case 2442/1997, No. 112, volume XXVIII, case 9592/1998 and permit for use 9100/1/-1998 submitted by the SELLER.

1.2. The BUYER buys from the SELLER the real estate property, described in clause 1.1 for the amount of 60,000 EUR in return for gaining the property rights upon the real estate described in clause 1.1.

II.   RIGHTS AND OBLIGATIONS OF THE PARTIES

2.1.   The SELLER undertakes to transfer to the BUYER the property rights upon the real estate described in clause 1.1 in the term until 31.03.2004. The possession of the property is transferred in the due term of day from supplying the SELLER with a Notarial deed.

2.2.   The SELLER undertakes to transfer to the BUYER the possession of the real estate described in clause 1.1. The condition of the real estate property at the moment of possession transfer is the same as at the moment of concluding the present contract; and namely: empty apartment with everything fitted to the property including: extractor fan fixed level, electric socket covers fixed flushed, all doors / windows open / close properly, handles for the windows to be fitted, new switches for the lights, new handles for the inside doors, cleaning the paint under the windows; according to a Description protocol /inseparable part of the present contract, in which condition of the property and furniture are described.

2.3.   The SELLER declares that there are no burdens upon the real estate, described in clause 1.1, and that there are no restraints imposed, mortgages outstanding, real rights, etc. The SELLER undertakes not to conclude preliminary contracts for sale trade with other persons and not to mortgage the real estate described in clause 1.1 until final witnessing of the transaction before a Notary Public is made.

2.4.   The BUYER undertakes, on signing this contract, to pay as a part of the deposit to the SELLER in advance the amount of 2,000 EUR and the same should be paid to the SELLER in return for a receipt, representing part of the sale price of the estate.

2.5.   The BUYER undertakes to transfer the rest of the deposit of 4,000 euro until 19.02.2004.

2.6.   The BUYER is obliged to deposit to the SELLER the rest of the sum, fixed by clause 1.2 of the present contract, i.e. 54,000 EUR in the mentioned by the SELLER bank account or in cash.

III.   RESPONSIBILITIES AND SANCTIONS

3.1.   The SELLER is obliged to return to the BUYER the paid in advance sum, pointed out in clause 2.4 and 2.5 of the present contract, of 6,000

EUR, in its double amount, namely 12,000 EUR in its BGL equivalence by the fixing of the Bulgarian National Bank on the day of payment in favour of the SELLER if he / she does not perform exactly, and in due time, the undertaken obligations, according to the present contract.

3.2. The BUYER loses the paid in advance sum fixed by clause 2.4 of the present contract – handset amount, of 6,000 EUR in favour of the SELLER if he / she does not perform exactly and in due time the undertaken obligations according to the present contract.

IV. GENERAL TERMS

4.1. The parties under the present contract agree that the expenses incurred for the transfer of the real estate as per item 1.1 of the present contract are on the account of the BUYER.

4.2. All additional agreements between the parties in connection with the present contract are to be made in written form only and will be considered an integral part of this contract.

4.3. The action of the present contract cannot be terminated unilaterally. It is to be terminated only on the mutual consent of both parties in writing.

4.4. For any matters not settled by the present contract the provisions of the Law for the Obligations and Contracts and the Civil Procedure Code are to be applied.

The present contract has been signed in the presence of a representative of 'ACME BULGARIA HOLDING' Ltd and was made in three identical copies – one for each of the parties and one for 'ACME BULGARIA HOLDING' Ltd.

SELLER   BUYER

1. ....   1. ....
/name, signature/   /name, signature/

2. ....   2. ....
/name, signature/   /name, signature/

Of 'ACME BULGARIA HOLDING' Ltd. ....
                              /name, signature / stamp

APPENDIX O: SAMPLE RECEIPT FOR DEPOSIT PAYMENT

RECEIPT

FOR DEPOSIT PAID

Today, the 06.02.2004 in the town of Varna, hereunder signed:

1. Nick Dobranov, Personal No. 1234567890 – Varna

2. Emil Dobranov, Personal No. 2345678901 – Varna

SELLER of a property in the town of Varna, 14 'General Tsankov', garret living floor **received from the BUYER**

1. John Smith, date of birth 08.07.1968; Passport number No. 345678901, issued 23.12.1996

2. Maria Jane, date of birth 15.03.1977; Passport number No. 456789012, issued 07.02.1997

2,000 Euro that represents to pay as a part of deposit, declared in Part II, point 2.4. of the preliminary contract for the sale trade of a real estate, concluded on 06.02.2004

The above mentioned sum I received in cash.

SELLER

3. ....
/name, signature/

4. ....
/name, signature/

Of 'ACME BULGARIA HOLDING' Ltd. ....
                    /name, signature, stamp/

Notary fee according to the Notary Law Stated Material Interest amounting to:		Entry as per The MS / PV Law Official Entries Office
Xxx BGL		Re No: 1450/03.02.2004
Proportional fee	268.50 BGL	Deed No: 69 File No: 1014/04
Usual fee	6.00 BGL	Lot re . Book: vol.... . 26210
Additional fee		Ent due fee
Total:		Receipt No: 40
Account No : 6130, year 2004		Judge on Official Entries: Signed Iill./ at Round Seal of the Official Entries Office Varna Regional Court duly affixed.

APPENDIX P: SAMPLE FINAL CONTRACT

<u>NOTARY DEED</u>

for

SELLING-PURCHASING OF A REAL ESTATE

No: 115 Volume: I Reg.No: 1287 File No: 94; year 2004

On this 3rd /Say: third/ February 2004, in the city of Varna, before me, ALEKSANDER VASILEV, Notary Public registered under No: 194 in the register of the Notary Chamber, Sofia city, active within the region of Varna Regional Court, in my Notary Office in the city of Varna, 36, Dragoman str., the following individuals presented: **NICK DOBRANOV**, Personal civil No: 1234567890; permanent residence in the city of Varna, and **EMIL DOBRANOV**, Personal civil No: 2345678901; permanent residence in the city of Varna on one side, in their capacity of the '**SELLERS**' and **JOHN SMITH**, citizen of the United Kingdom of Great Britain and Northern Ireland; born on 8th July, 1968, in Sutton in Ashfield; holder of Passport No: 345678901, issued on 23rd December, 1996; **in person and as a proxy for MARIA JANE** citizen of Estonia, born on 15th March, 1977, in Tallinn, holder of personal Passport No: 456789012, issued on 7th February, 1997, on the other side in the capacity of the '**BUYERS**'; and in the presence of the translator Ralitza Ranguelova, Personal civil No: 567890123 from the city of Varna, and having made sure of their identity, abilities and representing powers, the parties have stated that they conclude hereby the following contract:

1/ NICK DOBRANOV, and EMIL DOBRANOV sell to JOHN SMITH and MARIA JANE, their own real estate, namely:

FLAT No: 1 (Say: first); in a non-finished state, located in the city of Varna, Varna district, in the residential area 'St Nikola-4', on the attic floor in entrance '**A**' of a residential building under construction on RLP 9- (Say: ninetieth) in residential district 50 (Say: fifty), as per the lay-out of 21st (Say: twenty first) sub-region in the city of Vama, with area of the flat 111.90 sq.m. (Say: one hundred and eleven square meters and ninety hundredths), comprised of: an entrance lobby, a living room with a small kitchen, two bedrooms, a bathroom — toilet, a terrace, with boundaries as follow: flat No: 17 (Say: seventeenth), a street, a courtyard, 'Shipka' restaurant, together with the appurtenant cellar No: 17 (Say: seventeenth), with area of 2.08 sq.m. (Say: 2 square meters and eight hundredths), with boundaries: cellar No: 16 (Say: sixteenth), a corridor, staircase, and including the 4.6083 per cent (Say: four, point six thousand and eighty three) ideal shares out of the common parts of the building and of the right to construction owned by entrance '**A**', for the price of 60,000 BGL/Say: sixty thousand Leva/, which price has been fully paid by the Buyer, represented by their proxy, in favour of the Seller.

The **TAX EVALUATION** of the real estate described herein, is 33,626.85 BGL (Say: thirty three thousand, six hundred and twenty six leva, eighty two stotinki).

2/ The Buyers, **JOHN SMITH** and **MARIA JANE,** have stated that agree and buy the real estate described in p.1 of the present contract, for the price stated and fully paid to the Seller by the day of signing the present contract and under the terms and conditions described in details in an additional Agreement which shall be an inseparable part of the present Notary Deed.

3/ At signing the present Notary Deed, both contracting parties have agreed that in case of court suspension of the Buyers or at other cases that would cause the loss of their ownership rights over the real estate described in p.1 above, the Sellers will pay in their favour a forfeit amounting to three times the purchase price paid by the Buyers.

After I have been assured that the Sellers are the legitimate owners of the real estate and that all the particular requirements of the Law have been met, the parties have explained in front of me their resolution and actual status and have confirmed that they are fully aware of the legal consequences thereof, and with a view to protecting my rights and interests, I have drawn up this Notary Deed. The Notary Deed has been read to the parties, and after its respective approval, it has been duly signed by them and by me, the Notary Public.

At drawing up of the present Notary Deed written evidences were presented to verify the right of ownership of the seller and the observance of the particular requirements of the Law, as follows:

1. Notary Deed for selling of a real estate, No: 20, volume I, Reg. No: 419, file No: 18 from 1st March, 2002, issued by Georgi Ivanov — Notary Public with area of activity within Varna Regional Court;

2. Notary Deed for selling of a real estate, No: 21, volume /1, Reg. No: 424, file No: 19 dated on 1st March, 2002, issued by Georgi Ivanov — Notary Public with area of activity within Varna Regional Court;

3. Application in conformity with Art. 183 from the ZUT, entered in the Official Entries Office on 7th May, 2002, in vol.VJI, N2 28, register 5775;

4. Construction Licence #67/30.03.2001, issued by Varna Municipality, 'Primorski' region;

5. Lay-out draft No: #AB-94 G-154/12.06.2003, issued by Varna Municipality, 'Primorski' region;

6. Certificate for tax evaluation as per Art.226 of the SPC with reg.No: 529 dated on 19.01.2004, issued by Primorski Tax Administration Branch Office at Varna Tax Administration Head Office;

7. Declarations as per Art.226, par.1 from the SPC – 4 pcs.;

8. Declaration as per Art. 25 from the Notary Law;

9. Receipt for local tax duly paid in the amount as envisaged by Art.47, par.2 from the Local Taxes and Fees Law;

10. Receipt for official entry governmental fee, duly paid.

The sworn translator, after being reminded about the responsibility as per Art.290 from the Penalty Code, translated to the Buyers the text of the present Notary Deed into English language and stated that they understand it and that they agree with it.

SELLERS: 1. *Signed*   BUYERS: 1. *Signed*

2. *Signed*   2. *Signed*

SWORN TRANSLATOR:
Signed

NOTARY PUBLIC *Signed*

Round Seal of the Notary Public Aleksander Vasilev affixed.

I, the undersigned RALITZA RANGUELOVA, do hereby certify and attest that the translation of the hereto attached document — Notary Deed No: 115, rendered by me from Bulgarian language into English language, is truly and genuinely that of the Original. The translation consists of three (3) pages.

Certified Translator:

Ralitza Ranguelova Civil ID No: 567890123

APPENDIX Q: SAMPLE RENTAL MANAGEMENT CONTRACT

Today, on this..........day of..............of the year 2004, in the town of Varna the present contract was signed by and between:

1. **JOHN SMITH**, citizen of the United Kingdom of Great Britain and Northern Ireland, born on 08.07.1968 in Sutton-in-Ashfield, Great Britain, holder of passport GBR No. 12345678901, issued on 23.12.1996 by the passport authorities of Great Britain, valid until 23.12.2006 and,

2. **MARIA JANE**, citizen of Republic of Estonia, born on 15.03.1977 in Tallinn, holding passport No. 23456789012, issued on 07.02.1997, valid until 07.02.2007, hereinafter referred to as the Clients, forming one party and

3. **'ACME PROPERTIES VARNA' LTD**, registered under court file No. 152/2004 of the inventory of the County Court of Varna – Company Department, domicile and registered office: town of Varna, region 'Odesos', 17 'General Curie', floor 2, Bulstat No. 98765432, tax No. 1234174628, represented by its manager Mila Dobrova, Personal ID No. 1111222233, hereinafter referred to as the Agent, forming the other party

The parties have agreed on the following:

I. SUBJECT OF THE CONTRACT

The Clients entrust and the Agent undertakes the obligation to perform deals of management, in 3 /three/ months term, in relation to the real estate owned by the Clients as follows: APARTMENT No. 1 /one/, situated in the town of Varna, county of Varna, 'Sveti Nikola-4' region, on garret floor, entrance '1', with total area of 111.90 /one hundred eleven point ninety/ sq.m., consisting of: entrance-hall, living room with kitchen, three bedrooms, bathroom, toilet and a terrace:

♦ to conclude leases on the Clients' behalf and account, to pay the current expenses in relation to the use of the above real estate, including expenses for the cleaning of the real estate, current repairs, etc.

- to conclude on the Clients' behalf and account insurance contracts, as well as contracts with enterprises performing security services.

- to represent the Clients before any physical and juridical persons and thus to perform any required actions on the Clients' behalf and account, as well as to sign any contracts and other papers in relation to the above real estate excluding the sale of any real estate or part thereof.

- to represent the Clients at the preparation, giving and receiving of any documents and sums in relation to the performance of the above actions.

- to organize the meeting of the tenants, their transportation and their accommodation in the property.

2. The Agent hereby undertakes to perform the assignment on behalf and on the account of the Clients;

3.1) The Clients hereby undertake to pay to the Agent the remuneration as follows:

a) In cases when the above property is not rented with the agency of the Agent:

- 15 /fifteen/ euro for every meeting and/or dispatch of tenants;

- 25 /twenty five/ euros per week for cleaning of the property;

- the needed amount for eventual small repairments;

b) In cases when the above property is rented with the agency of the Agent:

- 20 per cent /twenty per cent/ of the sum, which includes the expenses for the maintenance of the real estate and the pick up and return of the tenants.

c) In cases when the above property is not rented at all:

10 /ten/ euro per week – for cleaning and maintenance of the property;

3.2) The payment received by the Agent, under the above contracts, shall be paid to the Clients, personally to them or to an authorized by them representative, in cash or by bank remittance to a bank account, designated by the Clients, after the deduction of the remuneration agreed on in section I, item 3.1) hereof and after the deduction of the expenses, made by the Agent, calculated with all the invoices for those expenses.

II. RIGHTS AND OBLIGATIONS OF THE CLIENTS

4. The clients shall be obliged:

    a) to provide the required data and information for the performance of the assignment;

    b) when requested to provide for the Agent money in advance for the performance of the assignment;

    c) to pay to the Agent the remuneration agreed on in section I, item 3.1);

    d) to pay to the Agent the amount of the expenses made in relation to the performance of the assignment together with the interests due, as well as the damages, suffered by the Agent in relation to the performance of the assignment;

    e) to give a one-day prior notice to the Agent of their intention to use the above real estate.

    f) to inform the Agent immediately if the property is rented without his agency by the phone or by email.

5. The clients shall have the following rights:

    a) to require reporting information about the performance of the assignment at any time;

    b) to receive an account of the performance of the assignment and everything which the Agent has received for the performance of the assignment.

III. RIGHTS AND OBLIGATIONS OF THE AGENT

6. The agent shall have the following obligations:

    a) to perform the assignment with the due care and attention and to protect the Clients' interests;

    b) to notify the Clients immediately of the results of the performance of the assignment;

c) to notify the Clients immediately if the property is rented out by phone or by email;

d) to give to the Clients everything which he has received under the deal;

e) to protect the property which he receives by the Clients or by third parties in relation to the performance of the assignment;

f) to produce a full inventory of items within the property.

7. The Agent shall have the following rights:

a) to re-authorize other people with the rights hereof and the Power of Attorney only with the explicit consent of the Clients or if this is necessary in order to protect the Clients' interests.

b) to sign, receive and give any documents on the Clients' account in relation to the performance of the assignment;

c) at the prompt performance of the assignment to receive the agreed on remuneration;

d) to perform any other required legal actions in relation to the performance of the present contract.

IV. TERMINATING AND BREAKING THE CONTRACT

8. The present contract shall be terminated at:

a) the death or the limited ability of any of the parties

b) withdrawal of the assignment by the Clients;

c) refusal of the Agent to perform the assignment;

d) expiration of the specified term

9. 1) When the Clients withdraw the assignment, they shall owe to the Agent a part of the agreed fee and payment of the made expenses.

2) If the performance of the assignment is impossible due to reasons for which the parties are not responsible, the Clients shall be obliged to pay to the Agent the expenses made by the latter and the relevant part of the remuneration.

10. If the Agent refuses to perform the assignment without notifying the Clients of that, he shall be obliged to pay an indemnification to them for the incurred damages and a penalty to the amount of 50 /fifty/ EURO.

11. The Clients shall have the right to break the present contract if:

    a) The Agent does not begin the performance of the assignment within one month after the present contract is signed

    b) The Agent does not perform an important part of his assignment under the agreed way.

12. The Agent shall have the right to break the contract hereof if:

    a) The Clients have provided untrue information and the performance of the assignment was impossible;

    b) The Clients do not pay the remuneration due within 7 days of receiving notification that payment is due.

V. FORFEITS

13. If the Clients do not fulfil their obligation to pay the remunerations and expenses agreed on in the present contract, they shall pay to the Agent a forfeit to the amount of 1 per cent of the sum for each overdue day.

14. If the Agent does not perform the assignment according to the way agreed on in the present contract, the Agent shall pay a forfeit to the amount of 1% of the stipulated remuneration.

VI. ADDITIONAL CLAUSES

15. For anything which is not provided hereof, the regulations of the Law of the Obligations and Contracts and the active legislation shall apply.

16. The parties shall settle the disputes which may arise at the fulfillment of the present contract by mutual agreement, and if this is not possible – under the Civil Procedure Code.

The present contract was signed in two identical copies – one for each of the parties.

The Clients: 1.------------------------

                      2.------------------------

The Agent: ------------------------

APPENDIX R: SAMPLE POWER OF ATTORNEY FOR RENTAL MANAGEMENT COMPANY

POWER OF ATTORNEY

We, the undersigned:

1. JOHN SMITH, citizen of the United Kingdom of Great Britain and Northern Ireland, born on 08.07.1968 in Sutton-in-Ashfield, Great Britain, holder of passport GBR No. 12345678901, issued on 23.12.1996 by the passport authorities of Great Britain, valid until 23.12.2006, and

2. MARIA JANE, citizen of Republic of Estonia, born on 15.03.1977 in Tallinn, holding passport No. 23456789012, issued on 07.02.1997, valid until 07.02.2007,

HEREBY AUTHORIZE

MILA DOBROVA, Personal ID No. 1111222233, ID Card No. 87654321, issued on 16th August 2000 by the Ministry of Interior – Varna

To perform any management activities with our own real estate: APART-MENT No. 1 /one/, situated in the town of Varna, county of Varna, 'Sveti Nikola-4' region, on garret floor, entrance 'A', with total area of 111.90 /one hundred eleven point ninety/ sq.m., consisting of: entrance-hall, living room with kitchen, two bedrooms, bath-toilet and a terrace, as the examples enumerated below do not limit the performance of other management activities:

◆ to conclude on our behalf and on our account leases with people and at prices at his own discretion, to prolong and terminate the term of such contracts, as well as to receive the rent;

◆ to pay on our behalf and on our account the current expenses in relation to the use of the above real estate, including such expenses related to the cleaning of the property, current repairs, etc.;

◆ to conclude on our behalf and on our account insurance contracts, as well as contracts with enterprises performing security services, with people and under conditions at his own discretion, to prolong and terminate the term of such contracts, as well as to give and receive the sums being insurance compensations or other payments under these contracts;

◆ to conclude on our behalf and on our account contracts with people and at a price agreed with the Client, to perform any needed actions, to receive and sign any needed documents in relation to the furnishing and equipment with furniture and equipment of the above real estate.

◆ to represent us before any authorities of the state and municipal administration (the Customs, the Sanitation and Epidemiologic Inspectorate, the State Veterinary Sanitary Control, the National Insurance Institute, the National Statistic Institute, etc.), and thus to perform any required actions, to receive and sign all needed documents on our behalf and on our account in relation to the above real estate.

◆ to represent us before the officials of the Taxation Administration and thus to perform any required actions, to receive and sign all needed documents, to prepare, sign, file and receive any declarations, certificates, AUAN on our behalf and on our account in relation to the above real estate.

◆ to represent us before any juridical (the Water Supply Company, the Power Supply Company, the Bulgarian Telecommunication Company, Bulgarian Posts, etc.) and physical bodies and thus to perform any required actions on our behalf and on our account, as well as to sign all contracts and other papers in relation to the above real estate excluding the sale of any real estate or part thereof.

Authorizers: 1.-------------------------
                 /John Smith/

                 2.-------------------------
                 /Maria Jane/

APPENDIX S: BULGARIAN EMBASSIES ACROSS THE WORLD

AUSTRALIA, SYDNEY
Consulate General of the Republic of Bulgaria

4 Carlotta Road,
Double Bay N.S.W. 2028
PO Box 1000, Double Bay, NSW, 1360
Tel: (0061 2) 932-77-581(consul)
932-77-592 (staff members)

tel/fax:	(0061 2) 9327 8067
e-mail:	bulcgsyd@bigpond.com
website:	www.users.bigpond.com/bulcgsyd

BELGIQUE, BRUXELLES 1180
Ambassade de la Republique de Bulgarie

58, Avenue /Hamoir, UCCLE

tel:	(0032 2) 375-70-81, 374-47-88,
	374-59-61; 374-59-62; 374-59-63
fax:	(0032 2) 375-84-94
e-mail:	embassy@bulgaria.be

BELGIQUE, BRUXELLES B 1180
Mission de la Republique de Bulgarie aupres des Communnautes Europeennes

1180 Uccle
Av. Moscicki, 7

tel:	(0032 2) 375-22-34, 374-84-68, 374-27-65
fax:	(0032 2) 374-91-88
e-mail:	info@mission.be

BOSNIA AND HERCEGOVINNA, SARAJEVO 71000
Embassy of the Republic of Bulgaria

ul. Trampina br. 12/II

tel:	(00387 71) 668-191
tel/fax:	(00387 71) 668-189, 668-182
e-mail:	possar@bih.net.ba

BRASIL, BRASILIA D.F. 70 432
Embaixada da Republica da Bulgaria

Sen-Avenida das Naçoes, Lote 08
Brasilia D.F.

tel:	(0055 61) 223-6193
fax:	(0055 61) 323-3285
e-mail:	bulgaria@abordo.com.br
website:	bg_consul@abordo.com.br

BUNDESREPUBLIK DEUTSCHLAND, BERLIN 10117
Botschaft der Republik Bulgarien

Mauer Str.11

tel:	(0049 30) 201-09-22/23/24/25/26
tel/fax:	(0049 30) 208-68-38
e-mail:	bbotscaft@myokay.net

BUNDESREPUBLIK DEUTSCHLAND, 53173 BONN 2
Abenstelle der Botschaft der Republik Bulgarien

Bad Godesberg, Auf der Hostert 6

tel:	(0049 228) 36 30 61 /65/
fax:	(0049 228) 35-82-15
e-mail:	bulbot@aol.com

BUNDESREPUBLIK DEUTSCHLAND, 80638 MUNCHEN
General konsulat der Republik Bulgarien

Walhallstr. 7
80639 Munchen

tel:	(0049 89) 15 50 26/27
fax:	(0049 89) 15 50 06
e-mail:	genkonsulbg@aol.com

CANADA, OTTAWA, ONTARIO K1N 6K5
Embassy of the Republic of Bulgaria

325, Stewart Street

tel:	(001 613) 789-32-15, 789-35-23 (consul)
tel/fax:	(001 613) 789-35-24
e-mail:	mailmn@storm.ca

CANADA, TORONTO, ONTARIO M4H 1P1
Consulate General of the Republic of Bulgaria

65, Overlea blvd., Suite 406

tel:	(001 416) 696-24-20; 696-27-78
tel/fax:	(001 416) 696-80-19
e-mail:	bulcontor@primus.ca

CESKA REPUBLIKA, 11 000 PRAHA 1
Velvyslanectvi Bulharske Republiky

6, ul. 'Krakovska'

tel:	(00420 2) 2422-86-46/7/8, 222-10-230, 222-12-264
fax:	(00420 2) 2422-24-63
e-mail:	bulvelv@mbox.vol.cz

CHILE, SANTIAGO
Embajada de la Republica de Bulgaria

Calle Rodolfo Bentjerodt 4895

Las Condes – Vitacura

tel:	(0056 2) 228-31-10
fax:	(0056 2) 208-04-04
e-mail:	embul@entelchile.net

CHINA, BEIJING 100 600
Embassy of the Republic of Bulgaria

4, Xiu Shui Bei Jie

tel: (0086 10) 6532-1946, 653-219-16
fax: (0086 10) 6532-4502
e-mail: bulemb@public.bta.net.cn

CROATIA, 10 000 ZAGREB
Embassy of the Republic of Bulgaria

Novi Goljak, 25

tel: (0038 51) 455-22-88, 455-22-89
tel/fax: (0038 51) 455-34-78
e-mail: veleposlanstvo-bugarske1@zg.tel.hr

CUBA, LA HABANA
Embajada de la Republica de Bulgaria

Calle 'B' No. 252, Entre 11 y 13
Vedado, La Habana

tel: (0053 7) 33-31-25, 33-31-26, 33-31-29
fax: (0053 7) 33-32-97
e-mail: embulhav@ceniai.inf.cu

CYPRUS, NICOSIA, PC 1700 ENGOMI
Embassy of the Republic of Bulgaria

13, Constantinou Paleologou Str.
P.O. Box 4029

tel: (00357 2) 67-24-86, 67-27-40
fax: (00357 2) 67-65-98
e-mail: bulgaria@cytanet.com.cy

DENMARK, COPENHAGEN
Embassy of the Republic of Bulgaria

Gamlehave Àlle 7, 2920 Charlottenlund

tel: (0045 39) 64-24-84, 63-38-72
fax: (0045 39) 63-49-23
e-mail: bg-embassy@email.dk

EGYPT, CAIRO
Embassy of the Republic of Bulgaria

6, El Malek El Afdal Str. Zamalek

tel: (0020 2) 341-30-25; 341-60-77
fax: (0020 2) 341-38-26
e-mail: mka@link.com.eg

ESPANA, MADRID 28016
Embajada de la Republica de Bulgaria

Santa Maria Magdalena, 15

tel: (0034) 913-456-651; 913-455-761
fax: (0034) 913-591-201
e-mail: embulmad@teleline.es

FINLAND, 00340 HELSINKI 14
Embassy of the Republic of Bulgaria

Kuusisaarentie 2

tel: (00358 9) 458-40-55
fax: (00358 9) 458-45-50
e-mail: bulembfi@icon.fi

FRANCE, PARIS 75007
Ambassade de la Republique de Bulgarie

1, Àvenue Rapp

tel: (0033 1) 45 51 85 90, 45 55 97 44 (consul), 464-41-756
fax: (0033 1) 455-11-868
e-mail: bulgamb@wanadoo.fr

FRANCE, PARIS 75015
Delegation permanente de la Republique de Bulgarie aupres de l'UNESCO

1, rue Miollis

tel: (0033 1) 456-83-402
fax: (0033 1) 478-33-452

FRANCE, 67 000 STRASBOURG
Representation Permanente de Republique de Bulgarie

aupres du Conseil de l'Europe

22, rue Fischart

tel: (0033 388) 61-95-29, 61-13-40, 60-45-77
fax: (0033 388) 61-92-38; 41-18-02
e-mail: bulgarie@noos.fr

GREECE, ATHENS 154 52
Embassy of the Republic of Bulgaria

33 A, Stratigou Kallari Str.
Paleo Psychico, 15452

tel: (0030 1) 647-81-06; 647-81-07; 647-81-08
fax: (0030 1) 647-81-30
e-mail: embassbg@athserv.otenet.gr

GREECE, THESSALONIKI – 54643
Consulat General de la Republique de Bulgarie

Edmundo Abot No. 1

tel: (0030 31) 829-210; 829-211; 869-505; 869-510; 869-520
fax: (0030 31) 85-40-04
e-mail: gencosol@otenet.gr

HASHEMITE KINGDOM OF JORDAN, 11195 AMMAN
Embassy of the Republic of Bulgaria

um uzaina, Al-mousel street No. 7
P.O. Box 950578

tel:	(00962 6) 552-93-91, 553-93-92
fax:	(00962 6) 553-93-93
e-mail:	bulembjord@joinnet.com.jo

HUNGARIA, 1062 BUDAPEST VI,
Embassy of the Republic of Bulgaria

Andrassy st 115

tel:	(0036 1) 322-08-24, 322-08-36, 342-37-38
fax:	(0036 1) 322-52-15
e-mail:	bgembhu@attglobal.net

INDIA, NEW DELHI 110 021
Embassy of the Republic of Bulgaria

16-17 Chandragupta Marg,
Chanakyapuri

tel:	(0091 11) 611-55-51, 611-55-49, 611-55-50
fax:	(0091 11) 687-61-90
e-mail:	bulemb@mantraonline.com
website:	www.bulgariaembindia.com

INDONESIA, DJAKARTA 10310
Embassy of the Republic of Bulgaria

34-36, Jalan Imam Bonjol

tel:	(0062 21) 390-40-48-9
fax:	(0062 21) 390-40-49
e-mail:	bgemb.jkt@centrin.net.id

IRAQ, BAGHDAD
Embassy of the Republic of Bulgaria

Amiriyah, new diplomatic quarter
Mahala 624, Zukak 25, House 12

tel: (00964 1) 556-81-97; 555-530-15
fax: (009 641) 556-41-82
e-mail: bulgemb@uruklink.net

IRAN, TEHERAN
Embassy of the Republic of Bulgaria

Vali Asr Avenue, Tavanir
Nessami Ganjavi No. 82
P.O. Box 11365-7451

tel: (0098 21) 877-56-62; 877-50-37; 877-63-15
fax: (0098 21) 877-96-80
e-mail: bulgr.tehr@neda.net

ISRAEL, 62308 TEL-AVIV
Embassy of the Republic of Bulgaria

124, Ibn Gvirol Street, 9th floor

tel: (00972 3) 524-17-51; 524-17-59, 950-90-82
fax: (00972 3) 524-17-98
e-mail: bgemtlv@netvision.net.il

ITALIA, 00197 ROME
Ambassade de la Republique de Bulgarie

Via Pietro P. Rubens 21

tel: (003 906) 322-46-40; 322-46-43, 322-46-45; 322-46-48
fax: (003 906) 322-61-22
e-mail: bgamb.roma@tin.it

KAZAKHSTAN, 480002 ALMATY
Embassy of the Republic of Bulgaria

13-À, Makataeva str.

480002 Almaty

tel:	(007 3272) 30-27-54
tel/fax:	(007 3272) 30-27-55
tel/fax:	(007 3272) 30-27-49
e-mail:	dekov@ittå.kz

KINGDOM OF CAMBODIA, PHNOM PEHN
Embassy of the Republic of Bulgaria

Blvd.'Norodom' 227

tel:	(00855) 23-217-504, 15-915-825
fax:	(00855) 23-212-792
e-mail:	embabulg@forum.org.kh

KUWAIT, KUWAIT CITY
Embassy of the Republic of Bulgaria

Jabriya area 11, str.107 and str.1, House 31
P.O. Box 12090 – Shamia 71 651

tel:	(00965) 531-44-58, 531-44-59
fax:	(00965) 532-14-53
e-mail:	bgembkw@qualitynet.net

LEBANON, BEIRUT P.O.B. 11-6544
Embassy of the Republic of Bulgaria

55 Australia St., Sector 38, Hibri Bldg.
Raouche, Beirut, Lebanon

tel:	(009 611) 86-13-52
fax:	(009 611) 80-02-65
e-mail:	bgemb_lb@hotmail.com

MAROCO, RABAT
Ambassade de la Republique de Bulgarie
4 Avenue Ahmed El Yazidi /Ex
Meknes
P.O. Box 1301

tel:	(00212 7) 76-54-77; 76-40-82
fax:	(00212 7) 76-32-01

MEXICO C.D.F., MEXICO
Embajada de la Republica de Bulgaria
Paseo de La Reforma 1990
Lomas de Chapultepec
P.O. Box 41-505 Mexico d.f.-11001

tel:	(0052 5) 596-32-83, 596-32-95
fax:	(0052 5) 596-10-12
e-mail:	ebulgaria@yahoo.com

MONGOLIA, ULAN BATOR 13
Embassy of the Republic of Bulgaria
Olympic Str.Nî 8
P.O. Box 702

tel:	(00976 11) 32-97-21, 32-28-41 è 32-69-31
tel/fax:	(00976 1) 32-28-41
e-mail:	posolstvobg@magicnet.mn

NIGERIA, LAGOS
Embassy of the Republic of Bulgaria
3, Walter Carrington Crescent, Victoria
Island
P.O. Box 4441

tel:	(00234 1) 261-19-31, 61-19-32
fax:	(00234 1) 261-98-79
e-mail:	bulgarian@hyperia.com

NORWAY, 0244 OSLO
Embassy of the Republic of Bulgaria

Tidemands Gate 11

tel:	(0047 2) 255-40-40
fax:	(0047 2) 255-40-24
e-mail:	bulgemb@online.no

OSTERREICH, 1030 WIEN
Botschaft der Republik Bulgarien

Parkgasse 18
Tel: (0043 1) 713-31-64; 505-06-37;
505-25-57

tel/fax:	(0043 1) 713-43-40
telex:	131 749
e-mail:	bulembassy@eunet.at

OSTERREICH, WIEN 1040
Permanent Mission of the Republic of Bulgaria to the UN, OSCE and other International Organisations

Rechte Wienzeile 13

tel:	(0043 222) 585-20-02, 585-72-96, 586-72-96
fax:	(0043 222) 585-20-01
e-mail:	bulgvert@aon.at

PAKISTAN, ISLAMABAD
Embassy of the Republic of Bulgaria

Diplomatic Enclave
Plot 6-11, Ramna-5,
P.Î.Bîõ 1483

tel:	(0092 51) 227-91-967
fax:	(0092 51) 227-91-95
e-mail:	bul@isb.compol.com

PORTUGAL, LISBOA
Embaixada da Republica da Bulgaria

Rua do Sacramento a Lapa 31/33

tel: (00351 2) 397-76-364, 397-63-66
fax: (00351 2) 397-63-61
e-mail: ebul@mail.telepac.pt

REPUBLIC OF GHANA, ACCRA
Embassy of the Republic of Bulgaria

3 Kakramadu Road, East Cantonments
P.O. Box 3193

tel: (00233 21) 77-24-04
fax: (00233 21) 77-42-31
e-mail: bulembgh@ghana.com

REPUBLIC OF IRELAND, 4 DUBLIN
Embassy of the Republic of Bulgaria

22 Burlington Road

tel: (00353 1) 6603293
fax: (00353 1) 6603915
e-mail: bgemb@eircom.net

REPUBLIC OF KOREA, SEOUL 140-212
Embassy of the Republic of Bulgaria

723-42, HNNAM 2 dong, YONGSAN – ku

tel: (0082 2) 794-86-25, 794-86-26
fax: 794-86-27
e-mail: ebdy1990@unitel.co.kr

REPUBLIC OF MACEDONIA, 1000 SKOPIE
Embassy of the Republic of Bulgaria

3, Zlatko Shnaider str.

tel:	(003 89 91) 22-94-44, 11-63-20
fax:	(003 89 91) 11-61-39

REPUBLIC OF POLAND, WARSZAWA 00-540
Ambasada Bulgarii

Al. 'Ujazdowskie' 33/35

tel:	(0048 22) 629-40-71/72/73/74/75, 625-71-71
fax:	(0048 22) 628-22-71
e-mail:	office@bgemb.com.pl

REPUBLIKA SLOVENIJA, 1000 LJUBLJANA
Veleposlanistvo Republike Bolgarije

Jesenkova ul.2

tel:	(00386 1) 426-57-44
fax:	(00386 1) 425-88-45

ROMANIA, BUCHAREST, SEKTOR I
Ambassade de la Republique de Bulgarie

Strada Rabat No. 5, sec. 1

tel:	(0040 1) 230-21-50, 230-21-59
fax:	(0040 1) 230-76-54
e-mail:	bulembassy@pcnet.ro

SCHWEITZ, 3005 BERN 6
Botschaft der Republik Bulgarien

Bernastrasse 2-4

tel:	(0041 31) 351-14-55, 351-14-56
tel/fax:	(0041 31) 351-00-64
e-mail:	bulembassy@bluewin.ch

SLOVENSKA REPUBLIKA, BRATISLAVA-81106
Velvyslanectvo Bulharskej Republiky

Kuzmanyho 1/A

tel: (00421 7) 544-15-308, 544-35-971 (consulate)
fax: (00421 7) 544-12-404
e-mail: bulembas@stonline.sk

S.P.L.A JAMAHIRIYAH, TRIPOLI
Embassy of the Republic of Bulgaria

Talah Ben Abdula Str. No. 58-6
P.O. Box 2945

tel: (00218 21) 44-44-260, 44-44-279, 609-690
fax: (00218 21) 86-13-52
e-mail: bulem_lib@hotmail.com

SUISSE, GENEVE
Representation permanente de la Republique de Bulgariee aupres de l'Officie Europeen des Nations Unies et des Organisations internationales

Chemin des Crets-de-Pregny 16
1218 Grand Saconnex/Geneve
tel: (0041 22) 798-03-00, 798-03-01
tel/fax: (0041 22) 798-03-02
e-mail: bg.gecom@bluewin.ch
           bg.geneve@span.ch

SWEDEN, STOCKHOLM 11431
Embassy of the Republic of Bulgaria

Karlavägån 29

tel: (0046 8) 72-30-938; 79-05-942
fax: (0046 8) 21-45-03
e-mail: bg.embassy@ebox.tninet.se

SYRIE, DAMASCUS
Ambassade de la Råpublique de Bulgarie

Damascus Arnus Squar

Pakistan Street Buyl [1] 8, P.O. Box 2732

tel: (00963 11) 331-84-45, 445-40-39

fax: (00963 11) 441-98-54

e-mail: bul-emb@scs-net.org

THAILAND, BANGKOK 10110
Embassy of the Republic of Bulgaria

64/4 Soi Charoenmitr (Ekamai 10)

Sukhumvit 63 Prakhanong Nia,

Wattana

tel: (0066 2) 391-61-80, 391-61-81

fax: (0066 2) 391-61-82

e-mail: bulgemth@asianet.co.th

THE NETHERLANDS, 2597 HAGUE
Embassy of the Republic of Bulgaria

9, Duinroosweg, 2597 KJ The Hague

tel: (0031 70) 350-30-51

fax: (0031 70) 358-46-88

e-mail: bulnedem@xs4all.nl

TUNISIE, 1082 TUNIS
Ambassade de la Råpublique de Bulgarie

5, rue Ryhane, Citå Mahrajene -1082

P.O. Box 6

tel: (00216 1) 798-962, 796-182, 800-980, 785-790

fax: (00216 1) 791-667

e-mail: bgtunis.amb@planet.tn

TURQUIE, ANKARA
Ambassade de la Råpublique de Bulgarie

Atatu rk bulvari 124,
Kavaklidere

tel:	(0090 312) 42-67-455, 42-67-456
fax:	(0090 312) 427-31-78

TURQUIE, EDIRNE
Consulat Gånåral de la Råpublique de Bulgarie

Talat pasha bul. 31

tel/fax:	(0090 284) 214-06-17
e-mail:	bulgarkonsedn@ttnet.net.tr

TURQUIE, ISTAMBUL
Bulgaristan Baskonsoloslugu

Ahmet Adnan Saygun caddesi 44
Ulus-Levent 80600

tel:	(0090 212) 281-01-15
fax:	(0090 212) 264-10-11
e-mail:	bulgconsul@superonline.com
Website:	www.bulgarianconsulate-ist.org

UNITED KINGDOM OF GREAT BRITAIN AND NORTHERN IRELAND,
Embassy of the Republic of Bulgaria

186-188 Queen's Gate, London SW7 5HL

tel:	(0044) -(0) 207-584-9400; (0)207-584-9433
fax:	(0044) -(0) 207-584-4948
e-mail:	bgembasy@globalnet.co.uk

USA, NY 10028, NEW YORK
Permanent Mission of the Republic of Bulgaria to UNO

11, East 84th Street, NY 10028, USA

tel:	(001 212) 737-4790/91, 327-4080/81
fax:	(001 212) 472-98-65
e-mail:	bulgaria@un.int

USA, NY 10021, NEW YORK
Consulate General of the Republic of Bulgaria
121 East 62nd Street, NY 10021, USA

tel:	(00212) 935 46 46, 935 7920, 935 7938
fax:	(00212) 319 5955
e-mail:	bulconsgen@cs.com

USA, WASHINGTON DC 20 008
Embassy of the Republic of Bulgaria
1621 22nd Street, NW, Washington DC 20008,USA

tel:	(001 202) 387-0174; 387-0365; 483-1386
fax:	(001 202) 234-79-73
e-mail:	office@bulgaria-embassy.org
	bulgaria@iamdigex.net
website:	www.bulgaria-embassy.org

Consular Office, tel: 387-7969

e-mail:	consulate@bulgaria-embassy.org

VATICANO, ROME 00191
Ambasciata della Republica di Bulgaria presso la Santa Sede
Via Ferdinando Galiani, 36

tel:	(0039 6) 36-307-712
fax:	(0039 6) 32-92-987

VENEZUELA, CARACAS – 1060
Embajada de la Republica de Bulgaria

Calle 'Las Lomas', Quinta 'Sofia',
Urbanización – Las Mercedes
Apartado Postal: 68389

tel:	(0058 2) 993-27-14; 993-48-52
fax:	(0058 2) 993-48-39
e-mail:	embulven@cantv.net

VIETNAM, HANOI
Ambassade de la Republique de Bulgarie

'Van Phuc'

tel:	(0084 4) 846-08-56, 845-64-53; 845-29-08
e-mail:	bulemb@hn.vnn.vn

YEMEN, SANAA
Embassy of the Republic of Bulgaria

Area 'Asr', 4th str., Residence N 5
P.O. Box 1518

tel:	(00967 1) 20-84-69; 20-61-64
fax:	(00967 1) 20-79-24

ZIMBABWE, HARARE
Embassy of the Republic of Bulgaria

15, Maasdorp Avenue, Alexandra Park
P.O. Box 1809; 2758

tel:	(00263 4) 730-509
tel/fax:	(00263 4) 732-504
e-mail:	bgembhre@ecoweb.co.zw

APPENDIX T: FLIGHTS FOR 2008

Flights to Burgas

Flying from	Dates	Airline	Internet booking
Aberdeen	May – October	Balkan Holidays Air	www.balkanholidays.co.uk
Belfast	May – October	Balkan Holidays Air	www.balkanholidays.co.uk
Birmingham	25/5 – 28/9	Thomson Flights	www.thomsonfly.com
Birmingham	May – October	Balkan Holidays Air	www.balkanholidays.co.uk
Bristol	May – October	Balkan Holidays Air	www.balkanholidays.co.uk
Cardiff	25/5 – 5/10	Thomson Flights	www.thomsonfly.com
Cardiff	May – September	Balkan Holidays Air	www.balkanholidays.co.uk
Cork	May – September	Sunway	www.sunwayholidays.co.uk
Cork	May – October	Budget Travel	www.budgettravel.ie
Doncaster Sheffield	25/5 – 28/10	Thomson Flights	www.thomsonfly.com
Doncaster Sheffield	May – October	Balkan Holidays Air	www.balkanholidays.co.uk
Dublin	May – October	XL Airways	ie.xl.com
Dublin	May – October	Direct Holidays	www.directholidays.ie
Dublin	May – October	Budget Travel	www.budgettravel.ie
Durham Tees Valley	25/5 – 28/9	Thomson Flights	www.thomsonfly.com
Durham Tees Valley	May – October	Balkan Holidays Air	www.balkanholidays.co.uk
Dublin	May – September	Sunway	www.sunwayholidays.co.uk
East Midlands	29/5 – 25/9	Thomson Flights	www.thomsonfly.com
East Midlands	May – October	Balkan Holidays Air	www.balkanholidays.co.uk
Edinburgh	May – October	First Choice	www.firstchoice.co.uk
Edinburgh	May – October	Balkan Holidays Air	www.balkanholidays.co.uk
Exeter	May – October	Balkan Holidays Air	www.balkanholidays.co.uk

Flying from	Dates	Airline	Internet booking
Glasgow	22/5 – 2/10	Thomson Flights	www.thomsonfly.com
Glasgow	May – October	First Choice	www.firstchoice.co.uk
Glasgow	May – October	Balkan Holidays Air	www.balkanholidays.co.uk
Humberside	May – October	Balkan Holidays Air	www.balkanholidays.co.uk
Knock	May – October	XL Airways	ie.xl.com
Leeds/ Bradford	May – October	Balkan Holidays Air	www.balkanholidays.co.uk
Liverpool	May – October	Balkan Holidays Air	www.balkanholidays.co.uk
London Gatwick	25/5 – 5/10	Thomson Flights	www.thomsonfly.com
London Gatwick	May – October	First Choice	www.firstchoice.co.uk
London Gatwick	May – October	Balkan Holidays Air	www.balkanholidays.co.uk
London Stansted	May – October	Balkan Holidays Air	www.balkanholidays.co.uk
London Luton	Year round	Wizz Air	www.wizzair.com
Manchester	25/5 – 5/10	Thomson Flights	www.thomsonfly.com
Manchester	May – October	First Choice	www.firstchoice.co.uk
Manchester	May – October	Balkan Holidays Air	www.balkanholidays.co.uk
Newcastle	22/5 – 2/10	Thomson Flights	www.thomsonfly.com
Newcastle	May – October	First Choice	www.firstchoice.co.uk
Newcastle	May – October	Balkan Holidays Air	www.balkanholidays.co.uk
Shannon	May – September	Sunway	www.sunwayholidays.co.uk

Flights to Varna

Flying from	Dates	Airline	Internet bookinga
Belfast	May – October	Balkan Holidays Air	www.balkanholidays.co.uk
Bristol	May – October	Balkan Holidays Air	www.balkanholidays.co.uk
Cardiff	May – October	Balkan Holidays Air	www.balkanholidays.co.uk
Doncaster Sheffield	May – October	Balkan Holidays Air	www.balkanholidays.co.uk
Dublin	June – September	Sunway	www.sunwayholidays.ie
East Midlands	4/7 – 5/9	Thomson Flights	www.thomsonfly.com
Edinburgh	May – October	Balkan Holidays Air	www.balkanholidays.co.uk
Glasgow	May – October	Balkan Holidays Air	www.balkanholidays.co.uk
Leeds Bradford	May – October	Balkan Holidays Air	www.balkanholidays.co.uk
London Gatwick	24/5 – 4/10	Thomson Flights	www.thomsonfly.com
London Gatwick	Year round	British Airways*	www.ba.com
London Gatwick	Year round	Bulgaria Air	www.air.bg
London Gatwick	May – October	First Choice	www.firstchoice.co.uk
London Gatwick	May – October	Balkan Holidays Air	www.balkanholidays.co.uk
Manchester	23/5 – 3/10	Thomson Flights	www.thomsonfly.com
Manchester	Year round	Bulgaria Air	www.air.bg
Manchester	May – October	First Choice	www.firstchoice.co.uk
Newcastle	May – October	Balkan Holidays Air	www.balkanholidays.co.uk
Southampton	May – October	Balkan Holidays Air	www.balkanholidays.co.uk

*British Airways offer four flights a week to Varna, on Mondays, Tuesdays, Wednesdays and Saturdays

Flights to Sofia

Flying from	Dates	Airline	Internet booking
Dublin	Year round	Bulgaria Air	www.air.bg
Edinburgh	Year round	British Airways	www.ba.com
London Gatwick	Year round	Hemus Air	www.hemusair.bg
London Gatwick	May – October	Balkan Holidays Air	www.balkanholidays.co.uk
London Gatwick	Year round	Bulgaria Air	www.air.bg
London Gatwick	Year round	Easyjet	www.easyjet.com
London Heathrow	Year round	British Airways	www.ba.com
London Heathrow	Year round	Hemus Air	www.hemusair.bg
London Luton	Year round	Wizz Air	wizzair.com
Manchester	Year round	British Aiways	www.ba.com
Manchester	Year round	Bulgaria Air	www.air.bg
Manchester	May – October	Balkan Holidays Air	www.balkanholidays.co.uk
Newcastle	Year round	British Airways	www.ba.com

Glossary

Act 15 A document which the owners of a building/apartment complex sign to accept their approval of the building/apartment complex – prior to the completion of the building.

Act 16 A document that effectively provides approval from various authorities (including electricity, water, fire, construction control etc.) that a building complies with the regulations.

BACS BACS is an organisation established and owned by the major UK banks so that funds can be transferred between banks for the settlement of payments. BACS payment works on a 3-day cycle: Day 1 – Submit payment; Day 2 – Processed by BACS; Day 3 – Funds in Bank.

BBCC The British Bulgarian Chamber of Commerce – promoting business between the United Kingdom and Bulgaria.

BGL This is an abbreviation for the Bulgarian national currency, the Leva. You may also see this referred to as BGN.

BGN See BGL.

Bulgarian standard In real estate this term generally refers to the average finish on an apartment built in Bulgaria. The basic shell of the apartment is complete, with walls dividing the rooms and PVC windows (typically) – but usually means that no bath/shower/toilet has been installed, no kitchen furniture or appliances have been installed and only the concrete floors are there (no tiles or wooden floorboards etc.)

Bulgarian National Standard See Bulgarian Standard.

CHAPS This is one of the largest real-time gross settlement (RTGS) systems in the world. The abbreviation represents the **C**learing **H**ouse **A**utomated **P**ayment **S**ystem. The CHAPS system enables you to tell your bank to make an immediate payment. You know for certain that payment will reach the recipient on the day the bank makes the payment.

EUR This is a common abbreviation for the euro currency. Real estate transactions in Bulgaria are more commonly conducted in euros.

First-line plot In real estate, this term generally refers to a coastal plot of land that runs to (or close to) the edge of the cliff. A plot that sits just behind would be referred to as a second line plot, and a plot of land behind that as the third line and so on. Due to the likelihood of unobstructed views from a first line plot of land, they tend to be more preferable and also more expensive.

Leva This is the monetary unit of Bulgaria. It is commonly shortened to lv and also referred to as BGL and BGN. There are 100 stotinki in 1 Leva.

Lichna Carta This is a personal card, for foreigners, that is required for long-term stays in Bulgaria.

Notary Deed This document declares you as the legal owner of property/land.

Notary Public This is an official who authorises documentation (including the preliminary contract and notary deed).

OOD This is the suffix that represents a limited liability company. It is the Bulgarian equivalent of 'Ltd.'

Power of Attorney A Power of Attorney is a legal instrument that is used to delegate legal authority to another. In Bulgaria, you can give power of attorney to your solicitor or property management company representative etc. to conduct financial transactions or sign documents etc. on your behalf.

The terms would be specified within the power of attorney document itself.

Preliminary contract The initial contract that you sign, to declare your intention to buy a property or land plot.

Red zone A term you will hear real estate agents use on the Black Sea Coast to refer to land regions that are susceptible to landslides and other seismic activity.

REMI Real Estate Market Index. An index formed in 2002 to gauge the price fluctuations of real estate in Bulgaria.

Stotinki Smallest unit of currency in Bulgaria – equivalent to one hundredth of a Leva.

Type 'D' visa This is a visa with a 90 day validity and is issued to those who intend to apply for a long-term stay in Bulgaria (non EU/EEA citizens).

Viewing trip A trip organised specifically for viewing properties (or land plots), usually between two to five days.

Index

Disclaimer

This book does not intend to offer a substitute for professional legal or financial advice. Whenever dealing with the purchase of property or land, one must always consult the relevant professional bodies to ensure that one is up to date with the current legislation.

The laws and regulations in Bulgaria do change, and one must always seek the most up to date advice before proceeding with the purchase. Whilst I have provided information and advice in this book, it is recognised that some of the procedures will change in time. You are therefore advised to always seek professional consultation.

There is no intention, on the part of the author or publisher to infringe on any legal copyright for any of the information contained within this book. The author has sought the copyright permission for any material that would be reasonably expected to have a copyright notice assigned to it.

Unless otherwise stated, all photographs contained within this book have been taken by the author, and any individual with a copyright claim must be aware that all these images were taken by the author on a digital camera, for which the original images are available.

All prices within this book, relating to the cost of labour, land, property or good/services were based on actual prices in 2008, and are subject to change in the future according to market forces.

The sample contracts provided in this book illustrate the typical content of various types of legal contracts and contracts with property management companies. The identities of the buyers and sellers as well as the addresses and other sensitive details are fictitious. It should also be noted that to be a legally binding contract in Bulgaria, the notary deed must be in the Bulgarian language (Cyrillic text). To assist the readers, the sample contracts have been translated into English to make it easier for the reader to familiarise themselves with the typical content.